to:

from:

your magical life

a young witch's guide to becoming happy, confident, and powerful

amanda lovelace

Illustrated by Raquel Aparicio

RP|KIDS
PHILADELPHIA

Running Press
Hachette Book Group
1290 Avenue of the Americas, New York, NY 10104
www.runningpress.com
@Running_Press

First Edition: September 2024

Published by Running Press Kids, an imprint of Hachette Book Group, Inc.
The Running Press Kids name and logo are trademarks of Hachette Book Group, Inc.

The Hachette Speakers Bureau provides a wide range of authors for speaking events.
To find out more, go to www.hachettespeakersbureau.com or email
HachetteSpeakers@hbgusa.com.

Running Press books may be purchased in bulk for business, educational, or promotional
use. For more information, please contact your local bookseller or the Hachette Book
Group Special Markets Department at Special.Markets@hbgusa.com.

The publisher is not responsible for websites (or their content) that are
not owned by the publisher.

Print book cover and interior design by Susan Van Horn.

Library of Congress Cataloging-in-Publication Data
Names: Lovelace, Amanda, author.
Title: Your magical life : a young witch's guide to becoming happy, confident, and
powerful / Amanda Lovelace.
Description: First edition. | Philadelphia : RP Kids, 2024. | Audience: Ages 8-12 |
Audience: Grades 4-6
Identifiers: LCCN 2023044836 | ISBN 9780762484157 (hardcover) |
ISBN 9780762484188 (ebook)
Subjects: LCSH: Witchcraft—Juvenile literature. | Magic—Juvenile literature.
Classification: LCC BF1571 .L68 2024 | DDC 133.4/3—dc23/eng/20231218
LC record available at https://lccn.loc.gov/2023044836

ISBNs: 978-0-7624-8415-7 (hardcover), 978-0-7624-8418-8 (ebook)

Printed in China

APS

10 9 8 7 6 5 4 3 2 1

to the sad young girl who
once thought herself magicless:

oh, my sweet autumn child,

you were wrong
in the most beautiful way.

Ask an adult before using
matches or lighting candles
or incense. Never leave a candle
unattended. Handle spell
supplies and tools carefully.
If you are not sure, ask for help
with spell directions.

contents

a note from the author

Hello there, reader!

Welcome to *Your Magical Life: A Young Witch's Guide to Becoming Happy, Confident, and Powerful.*

If you had told me when I was a kid that I would one day be writing a book like the one you now hold in your hands, I doubt I would have believed you. In fact, I probably would have laughed.

I had always been inexplicably drawn to witchy things, but most of the witchcraft books I picked up as a teen were intimidating as *hex*. They made magic seem extremely complicated, using a bunch of words and terms I didn't understand and requiring ingredients someone like me just didn't have access to.

Back then, my long-held dream of being a witch seemed way too unrealistic, so I turned my focus away from it for a while, thinking it was a waste of my time and energy.

It wasn't until I came across easy-to-digest, short-form online content that I finally felt brave enough to cast my very first spell. I started by taking something I was already doing every day—making and drinking coffee—and found a way to make it magical. (Yes, I'll teach you to do something similar!) For a long time, that was all I was brave enough for, but even that was enough to add some sparkle back into my eyes.

Fast-forward to now, and most of my days are filled with magic, both big and small.

(But mostly just small.)

While big, complicated spells can be fun, they certainly aren't required for someone to be a witch. Small and simple magic that doesn't stress you out is valid. Small and simple magic that makes your day-to-day just a little bit brighter is valid.

Luckily, much has changed since I was a young and aspiring witch. We now live in a world where witchcraft is trending everywhere, and where they sell beginner-friendly witchcraft books at most major department stores. This book, however, is the one I wish I had when I was an overwhelmed beginner, when I so desperately wanted a more experienced hand to hold while I figured it all out.

I never want anyone to feel as lost as I did, so you won't find anything too fancy or elaborate here—just a safe and understanding place where you can start building the witchcraft practice that's right for you.

By the time you reach the last page, I hope you will have allowed yourself the joy of making a little magic of your own.

Laced with love,
amanda

to the brim she was filled with
moonbeams & starlight,
which she consciously kept dim.

in her mind, it made sense,
for it was a lot easier to pretend
that she wasn't capable
of shining so much brighter.

if i could, i would go back & tell her,
"no one ever said making magic
was going to be easy."

—*living up to your fullest potential rarely ever is.*

PART I

the basics

"so, what makes a witch?"

Pop culture is absolutely filled with fictional witches, so when you hear someone say the word *witch*, your mind might immediately go to the Sanderson sisters from *Hocus Pocus*, or maybe even Ursula from *The Little Mermaid*.

They're all complicated yet amazing characters who are undoubtedly beloved by many (especially those of us in the queer community, who often see ourselves reflected in these magical outcasts), and their creators may have even been inspired by real witches, but they don't quite represent what witches in our world are actually like.

More often than not, actual witchcraft looks a lot less like summoning faraway objects with the sound of your voice and a lot more like summoning a little self-confidence from within.

Though every witch ultimately practices differently (wouldn't it be boring if all of us were the same?), for many, including myself, being a witch is about recognizing that we have the magic within to bring just about anything we want into existence. We don't just sit around and wait for life to happen to us—we step up and take matters into our own hands.

Where we once felt power*less*, we now feel power*ful*.

"can i be a witch?"

Short answer: yes.

Slightly longer answer: absolutely. Everyone has the potential to make their own magic. Whether or not you *choose* to call yourself a witch is entirely up to you.

witchy labels

Some people like to use specific labels to describe what kind of witch they are, such as a green witch (someone who works primarily with things like plants, flowers, and herbs to make their magic) or a sea witch (someone who works primarily with things such as sand, seawater, and seashells to make their magic).

Meanwhile, some use more specific labels like crystal witch (someone who primarily uses crystals to make their magic) or tarot witch (someone who primarily uses tarot cards to make their magic).

You don't have to label yourself right now.

You don't have to label yourself by the time you're done reading this book, either.

Honestly, you don't have to label yourself *ever*, if you don't feel called to.

Let yourself explore this new magical world first. If you *do* eventually decide to label yourself—perhaps because it helps you feel more connected to your practice—then that's awesome! Just know that it's okay to change your mind later; it's okay to keep the label, too.

baby witch

In recent years, *baby witch* has become a label that new witches use to describe themselves—*you* don't have to, but I want to let you know that it's an option.

In my own experience, using the baby witch label can be very limiting and disempowering. I used that term for myself for *waaay* too long, mostly because I felt like I wasn't good enough or experienced enough to call myself a witch, even though I most definitely was after a certain point (experienced, that is; I was always good enough, and so are you).

3

When I dropped the "baby" part and finally just started calling myself a witch, I felt like I had finally stepped into my true magic, unapologetically and without shame . . . but of course, everyone's different.

Moral of the story: if it doesn't make you feel good, don't do it!

on witches, pagans, and wiccans

There's often some confusion around the difference between being a witch, being a pagan, and being a Wiccan, which is understandable, so I thought I would clear it up a little!

- A witch—Someone who practices witchcraft, which often includes casting spells, taking part in rituals, and working in tune with nature. Witchcraft isn't necessarily religious. People of any religion (or lack thereof) can be witches.

- A pagan—Someone who practices a pagan religion. *Pagan* is an umbrella term that encompasses many nature-based religions. To oversimplify, pagans often honor more than one god and/or goddess (this is called *polytheism*) and many—but not all—pagans practice witchcraft and consider themselves witches.

- A Wiccan—Someone who follows the Wicca religion, a branch of paganism founded in the mid-1900s. Wiccans often (but not always) believe in a dual god and goddess and live by a set of principles called "The Wiccan Rede." Though many Wiccans practice witchcraft and call themselves witches, not all do.

Because of the popularity of Wicca in the late twentieth and early twenty-first centuries, Wiccan beliefs and traditions have influenced how many witches practice modern witchcraft today, even if they don't realize it. Though *Your Magical Life* is a book about witchcraft as I see it, not paganism or Wicca, you will definitely see some pagan and Wiccan influences, such as the Wheel of the Year (more on this later).

Still confused?

Like all Catholics are Christian, **all Wiccans are pagan.**

Like not all Christians are Catholic, **not all pagans are Wiccan.**

Though it often *is* the case, **not all pagans and Wiccans are witches** or practice magic.

Anyone can be a witch—not just pagans or Wiccans—regardless of their religion.

"white magic" vs. "black magic"

In the witchcraft community, you'll come across people who choose to use the phrase "white magic" to mean "good magic" and the phrase "black magic" to mean "evil magic."

That isn't okay.

It may seem inconsequential, but words hold a lot of weight. They reflect and influence our society, and we live in one filled with a lot of injustice. The racist implications of those phrases are not in line with my personal *or* witchcraft ethics, and therefore I choose not to use them.

I discourage you from using them as well.

If you want to know how to describe what kind of magic someone practices, why not just ask them? I'm sure it would make for an interesting conversation!

witchcraft & gender

When someone says the word *witch*, you might automatically assume they're referring to a woman.

Well, I'm here to tell you that people of all genders (because there are *way* more than just two!) can call themselves a witch—not just women, and certainly not just cis women.

When I said we *all* have magic within, I meant it.

In my opinion, being an ethical witch also means being an inclusive witch, and it's not very kind to leave so many of your fellow witches out of the conversation. Doing so may make them feel like they don't belong in the community, and *everyone* deserves to feel a sense of belonging.

Be that safe space for every witch.

In what ways can you be more inclusive in your everyday life, and how can you extend that to your magical practice?

not being accepted

Thanks to its popularity on all major social media platforms, witchcraft is becoming not only more and more popular but more and more *understood*.

Sadly, despite that, some still refuse to open their hearts and minds to it.

Be warned that there are plenty of people out there who continue to believe the misconceptions that witchcraft is evil and that witches only ever have ill intent, even though that couldn't be further from the truth. They may even use harmful religious rhetoric to try to convince you that you're a bad person who's doing bad things.

Please know that you don't deserve any of it.

Don't *ever* be afraid to be your true self, no matter what anyone else says.

It may break your heart when the people you love don't accept you; the good news is that there *will* be tons of people who not only understand you but practice witchcraft, too, so be patient and don't give up hope!

Some people refer to concealing their witchy side from others for fear of judgment as *being in the broom closet*. I can't remember if I've ever used this term in the past—for a long time, I never thought too deeply about its meaning—but I've decided I definitely won't going forward. This phrase is clearly a spin on the idea of being in the closet as a queer person, and speaking from my experiences with both, the two can't be equated and I don't think it's appropriate to do so, though that's just one witch's opinion.

"how do i make magic?"

Most of the time, witches make their magic by casting something called— you probably guessed it—a spell!

You've almost certainly done something spell-like at least once before.

You know when you close your eyes and make a wish as you blow out your birthday candles every year? That's very similar to a manifestation ritual.

The difference is, when a witch casts a spell, they don't usually make a wish.

My spells usually start off with an intention in the form of a self-empowering affirmation. It's pretty painless to create one; all you have to do is take the thing you want to happen (e.g., something external like creating a beautiful art project, or something more internal like trusting yourself to make good decisions) or the thing you want to become (e.g., confident, inspired, or peaceful), and say it as though it's already true. That means you have to say it in the present tense.

As a witch, you wouldn't ask, "Can I *pretty please* remain strong through this difficult situation?"

No—you would firmly declare, "I am strong and can handle anything life throws at me, including this."

See the difference?

While words can certainly be effective by themselves, for a witch, what makes them even more so is combining them with things like actions and tools. The more energy and focus you put into your spell, the more powerful—the more *real*—it will become.

> Spells can be one-time things, but if you keep repeating that spell (or similar variations of it), then it becomes something called a *ritual*. (This is true of so many mundane daily activities, too. Do you drink juice every morning or eat a snack before bed every night? Those are rituals!) Rituals also tend to be a little more involved than your everyday spells, especially because they can be perfected and built upon over time.

your magical journal

Next, it's important that you start a magical journal. (You may hear some witches refer to this as a *grimoire* or a *Book of Shadows*, but I'll be referring to it as a *magical journal*.)

Honestly, any old notebook you have lying around will do, but I recommend getting a big binder if possible so you can easily add things and move them around.

Of course, it *is* the twenty-first century, and most of us are at least a little tech savvy, so you may instead choose to keep a "magical journal"

file going on a reliable computer, phone, or tablet if you have access to one. (No matter what anyone else says, a magical journal is *not* less magical just because it's electronic.) Your magical journal is a place where you can reflect upon where you are in your witchcraft journey as well as your life, take note of all the things you've learned (from this book and from others, as well as from any other sources you stumble upon, such as videos approved by your caregiver or information from witchy peers), and record details about things like spells, rituals, and tarot/oracle card readings.

You'll notice that I include magical journal prompts on some pages (including the one on page 6). These are intended to help you get the ball rolling on the self-reflection front. I hope that they'll inspire you to discover magic in every area of your life.

Having all of this information at your fingertips will make you a stronger witch over time—trust me.

If my experience is anything to go by, you'll likely have many magical journals over the course of your practice, so try not to put too much pressure on yourself to make your first one perfect. The way your craft *looks* isn't nearly as important as the way it makes you *feel*. Though it may be tempting, it's not necessary to go out and buy a hundred dollars' worth of stickers and pens to make it pretty. Be as realistic as possible and remember that you can still make it authentically *you* on a budget.

Think about the magical journey that lies ahead. What are you most excited about? What are you most afraid of? If you want, you can write your answers in your magical journal. If you do, make sure to come back to it at some point in the future so you can see just how far you've come.

your magical altar

In addition to your magical journal, you'll want to create your very first magical altar—a dedicated space where you can work your inner magic in the form of spells, rituals, divination, meditation, and more.

It can be anywhere: a bookshelf, a bedside table, a tray. It doesn't have to be anything too extravagant; just make sure it's clean and you have enough room to do your magic. (Keep in mind that you can always switch altar spaces later if you need to! You're not beholden to the first space you choose if you outgrow it or it's just not working for you anymore.)

Your inner magic is what makes all other magic possible, so it's only right that you place something on your altar to recognize and honor this part of yourself.

First, let me ask you this: *When you think of all the amazing things that you're capable of, what is it that you see?*

Perhaps it's an art piece you created.

Perhaps it's an award or a trophy for one of your achievements.

Perhaps it's a picture of yourself during one of your happiest moments, like a birthday or hanging out with friends.

Don't overthink this part too much!

The symbol of your inner magic can really be anything, as long as it's significant to you. Just go with the first thing you think of.

Whatever you decide on, go ahead and place it front and center on your altar because it's now going to be the focal point—*you* are going to be the focus, the center of it all.

Feel free to add things over time, or even switch them out periodically. I usually place the most recent book I've written or deck I've cocreated, replacing it once another has been published. My writing is part of my magic.

If you're stuck, ask yourself, "What's something that makes me proud to be me?" Freewrite (putting pen to page and writing continuously with no filter) for five minutes until you come up with something.

your magical tools

Magical tools give you a way to direct your inner magic. They help you bring it physically and energetically to life.

A good portion of your altar should be practical and suit your personal magical needs. On the next few pages are some basic tools you might want to consider stashing on, in, or around your altar. (It's helpful to have some drawers, shelves, and/or boxes nearby for this purpose.)

I know, I know, it seems like a lot, but try not to get too overwhelmed by this list.

These are all things you can obtain gradually over the span of your practice. If you need something and don't have the means to obtain it, then be a resourceful witch and substitute it with something you already have on hand.

For example, if you don't have a jar, that's fine, just clean and use an empty jam jar instead. If you don't have a clear quartz crystal, that's fine, too, just find and use a nice rock—those work the same and are (usually) free. Make your practice suit *you*, not the other way around.

"Welp, that should be good enough!" is basically my favorite phrase as a witch.

- Your magical journal

- A writing utensil

- Sheets of scrap paper—These will have endless uses, including writing down affirmations.

- A white candle—Considered by many to be the all-purpose candle because the color white contains every color. (Can't have an open flame in your home for whatever reason? Opt for a battery-operated candle instead!)

A lighter or matches—Used to light candles.

A candle snuffer—To safely put out your candles.

A candle wick trimmer—To trim your candle wicks before each and every use. (Untrimmed wick = large flame = danger!)

Whenever fire is involved in spellwork, make sure you use caution and follow fire safety, and always ask a caregiver for help.

Dried rosemary—Considered by many to be the all-purpose herb due to its myriad properties.

A clear quartz crystal—Considered by many to be the all-purpose crystal, as it can amplify any intention you give it.

Dried roses—Considered by many to be the all-purpose flower for the same reason rosemary is for herbs—So. Many. Magical. Properties! (Plus, they're very easy to find.)

Divination tools such as a tarot deck, an oracle deck, and/or a pendulum—For self-reflection and guidance, among other uses.

A bell—A great cleansing and protection tool.

Jars, cups, and bowls of all shapes and sizes—I can't even emphasize how many uses these have. For starters, you can store herbs and ingredients in them, and many spells are even contained within them.

Drawstring pouches—Like jars, cups, and bowls, you can store herbs and ingredients in them, and many spells are even contained in them—these are known as spell bags.

all-purpose tools

You probably noticed that I suggested a few all-purpose tools: a white candle to replace any candle, dried rosemary to replace any herb, a clear quartz crystal to replace any crystal, and dried roses to replace any flower.

You should be aware that there's been a lot of debate among witches about whether or not all-purpose tools should be encouraged, because, according to some, there are more specific and effective tools a witch could use instead.

Personally, I believe that the intention a witch has when using their tools as well as their own personal correspondences are what truly matters when it comes down to it. I also think that anything that makes someone's witchcraft journey just a little bit easier—especially at the beginning—should be seen as a positive thing.

You can consider these all-purpose tools a mere starting point, or a way to substitute whenever necessary.

It's up to you.

"personal correspondences?"

Yep!

Most magical tools have established magical correspondences that you can find in books or by doing an internet search. While I see the importance of them, I think a witch's personal correspondences are *way* more important.

You have thoughts and experiences that give you a unique perspective on the world, and that unique perspective is going to make your spells even more special and powerful, because your magic is ultimately tailored to *you*.

On the following pages, you'll find lists of established correspondences for tools like candles, herbs, and crystals that you can use as a reference when doing spellwork, but whatever you do, don't consider them your one and only holy grail.

Say that, for example, a happiness spell calls for a yellow candle because that's the established correspondence. Cool. But maybe when *you* think of happiness, you think of blue because of a specific memory you have of a fun day spent swimming in the ocean. Or maybe the color blue just makes you super-happy and you can't explain it. Use that instead!

your candles

White (all-purpose candle)—cleansing, peace, and protection

Black—anti-negativity, banishment, and protection

Gray—balance, calm, and rest

Red—confidence, self-empowerment, and strength

Pink—compassion, nurturing, and self-love

Orange—ambition, creativity, and justice

Yellow—intelligence, joy, and positivity

Green—growth, prosperity, and self-worth

Blue—healing, inspiration, and truth

Purple—intuition, magic, and wisdom

Brown—grounding, security, and stability

Gold—luck, power, and success

Silver—dreams, meditation, and self-reflection

Candles, as you probably know, come in various shapes and sizes. Some of the most popular among witches are tealight and chime candles, as they're smaller and tend to burn relatively quickly compared to larger types; however, you may use candles of any size, and you may find that you develop your own preference over time. Scented candles are fine, too, but it's even better when you use a scent that's associated with your spell's purpose.

One of the simplest spells you can do is to light a candle (again, remember to ask a caregiver for help with lighting candles) while saying an affirmation. For example, if you need a quick dose of self-love, you could light a pink candle and say something like, "I am as kind to myself as I am to other people." If you have time, let the candle burn all the way down; if not, go ahead and extinguish it (no, this won't mess anything up) and relight it whenever you have a chance.

your flowers & herbs

Rosemary (all-purpose herb)—cleansing, protection, and remembrance

Lavender—calm, intuition, and rest

Peppermint—abundance, healing, and luck

Rose (all-purpose flower)— beauty, love, and self-love

Chamomile—positivity, prosperity, and soothing

Cinnamon—energy, self-empowerment, and warmth

Bay leaves—banishment, manifestation, and money magic

Salt is always great to have on hand. Both table salt and sea salt can be used for any cleansing and protection. Pink Himalayan salt is great for gentle cleansing, especially in self-love spells. Black salt is great at helping keep negativity at bay.

Edible herbs and flowers can be added to your recipes or ready-to-eat food. (Always do your due diligence to make sure the ones you're using are safe to eat, like asking your caregiver.) Not only do they add flavor to your meal, but they also add their magical properties. For example, if you require a little boldness, sprinkle some cinnamon onto your toast or oatmeal while saying, "I am fearless in the pursuit of my goals today." Yup—it's really that easy!

your crystals

Clear quartz (all-purpose crystal)—clarity, cleansing, and healing

Rose quartz—beauty, gentleness, and self-love

Amethyst—calm, intuition, and wisdom

Most amethyst you'll be able to find comes in shades of purple, but my personal favorite is pink amethyst. I find that it inspires just enough self-love for me to be able to trust my intuition without hesitation. If you can get your hands on one, you might find it helpful if you have trouble trusting your intuition as well.

17

Citrine—ambition, joy, and manifestation

Black tourmaline—anti-negativity, anti-worry, and protection

Tiger's-eye—confidence, courage, and self-empowerment

Moss agate—abundance, grounding, and growth

Aquamarine—self-expression, tranquility, and truth

Rainbow fluorite—creativity, focus, and individuality

Rainbow moonstone (also called *white labradorite*)—harmony,
self-reflection, and new beginnings

When buying crystals, look for shops that source theirs ethically. If
you're not sure, ask the shop directly.

The simple act of carrying a crystal can be a spell. First, pick one
with energy you'd like to match and cleanse it (see pages 19–20). Next,
"charge" it with your intention by holding it and saying an affirmation.
For example, you might pick black tourmaline and say, "My worries
do not rule me, nor do they hold me back from having positive life
experiences." After, put it in your pocket or in a bag.

disappearing crystals

As you work more with crystals, you may notice that some will disappear.

For example, some years ago, I bought a beautiful twin clear quartz necklace from a small pop-up crystal shop in the mall.

Sadly, I ended up misplacing the necklace only a few months after wearing it nonstop. It was just . . . gone. Without a single trace. I searched my house high and low for years on end, never once coming across it. I *loved* this necklace, so I still think about it from time to time.

Though disappearing crystals may be frustrating, they can actually be a *good* thing.

I think some crystals find you when you need them the most and depart once you don't need them anymore. *Where* they go and *how* they go, I'm not so sure. You can decide for yourself what you want to believe. Some say it's faeries (a topic for a much different book), but who knows? I like to think they go to someone who needs their magic much more than you do.

Your crystals might break from time to time, too. If it's in an unusual or unexpected manner, that could also mean your crystal is done serving its purpose in your life. Regardless, if this happens, you can give it back to Mother Earth by burying it somewhere outside, or even in the soil of a potted houseplant.

cleansing your crystals

Everything has its own unique energy, including our magical tools. That's why we use them, after all—to complement and boost our spell's purpose!

However, they can also *pick up* extra energy from the people, places, and things nearby, and this energy isn't always going to be the most

19

uplifting or positive—it can sometimes be heavy or negative, or simply not vibe quite right with yours.

Not only that, but if they sit around for too long, their energy can become "stale."

Crystals, in my experience, have a particular knack for this kind of energy-shifting.

That's why I think it's so important that you magically cleanse them before using them in spellwork. In fact, there are several ways you can cleanse your crystals.

Sound cleansing—Can be done with an instrument such as a bell. Simply take it in hand and ring it around the crystal a few times. This should vibrate away any icky energy.

Moonlight cleansing—Can be done under the cleansing light of the full moon. You don't have to put your crystals outside; just leave them in a window that gets a lot of moonlight and move them in the morning. (Some crystals are sensitive to water, so make sure rain isn't in the forecast. Some can also become damaged by sunlight, so make sure you move them before sunrise.)

Wind cleansing—Can be done on a windy day. Put all of the crystals you want to cleanse into a bowl and place it somewhere in your yard. (Alternatively, you can cleanse a crystal using your breath—just blow the negative energy away like you would if you were wishing on a dandelion!)

cleansing yourself

It's time to learn how to cleanse your *own* energy.

Not only can cleansing your energy uplift your mood in general, it can also help you prepare before spellwork by removing any negative, unwanted, or stale energy attached to you that doesn't match the magic you're trying to create.

Cleansing can be really fun, too.

All you have to do is put on some Taylor Swift (or another artist of your choice) and start dancing. While you do so, your movements will shake off any "blah" energy.

If possible, try to do this for the length of one entire song!

> Your phone can collect all kinds of negative energy, and if it's always near you, like it is for so many of us, it can put you in a bad mood. For this reason, I highly recommend cleansing your phone at the beginning or end of each day. You can do this by ringing a bell around it like you would a crystal, or you can open up a playlist on your phone and put on a feel-good song—just leave it facedown somewhere and let those happy vibrations take care of it!

mother earth

Witches have a long-standing reputation of loving, respecting, and working with Mother Earth.

Not only does she provide us with life-sustaining resources such as food and water, but she also blesses us with heart-stopping beauty like forests and oceans. On top of that, she's super-magical, too. After all, where do you think we get the tools that help us with our spells—the herbs, the crystals?

That's right: from our ever-lovely and ever-generous Mother Earth.

She also made our very existence possible, and therefore our inner magic. It's no wonder so many witches try to do their part to take care of her and keep her thriving, especially in a time when she's at her most vulnerable due to our current climate emergency.

Here are a few ways *you* can do your part:

- Go low- or no-waste.

- Eat locally, vegetarian, or vegan.

- Go thrifting instead of buying new stuff.

- Sign earth-friendly petitions.

- Donate your time to environmental groups, or take part in a climate event (e.g., a nature cleanup).

- Keep up with political candidates who promise to take on climate change.

Try not to feel guilty if certain things aren't feasible for you for whatever reason; you are not a bad witch, I promise.

the pentacle

I wouldn't be surprised if you've been told that the pentacle—a five-pointed star enclosed in a circle—is a symbol of evil, as this is a very common misconception. In reality, pentacles are a symbol of Mother Earth. Each of the five points on the star represents one of her elements, and the circle surrounding it connects them all as one. For many witches, it's a sacred and protective symbol.

Each element has its own correspondences, including the following:

Earth—north | green | stability, nature, and prosperity

Fire—south | red | passion, creativity, and energy

Air—east | yellow | intellect, ideas, and communication

Water—west | blue | cleansing, emotion/intuition, and inspiration

> Just to be clear, *Mother Earth* encompasses the entire planet as well as her energy, whereas *earth* is just one of her elements.

You'll notice that the pentacle has a fifth element you may not have learned about before: spirit. Spirit can represent many things, but for the sake of this book, it represents you, the witch—your essence, your soul, your inner magic—working in complete and total harmony with the four other elements.

mother earth on your magical altar

You've already placed something on your altar to represent spirit—*you*.

Many witches, including myself, also choose to represent Mother Earth's four main elements on their altar as a way to honor our connection to one another, as well as to invite her magical energy into our spellwork.

Want to represent Mother Earth on your altar? Below are a few suggestions for things you can place there (and yes, use in your magic!). It's not required, but you can choose your items based on the element's corresponding color or place them in its corresponding cardinal direction.

- Earth—a crystal/stone, a jar of herbs, or deer/elf imagery

- Fire—a cauldron, a candle, or fox/phoenix imagery

- Air—a bell, a bowl of flower petals, or hummingbird/faerie imagery

- Water—a cup or mug, a seashell, or dolphin/mermaid imagery

Some witches place a cauldron on their altar to represent the element of water, as it's a vessel that can be filled with it. Personally, I only ever burn things in mine, so I associate it more with fire. Consider both perspectives and come to your own conclusion!

To connect with Mother Earth is, in many ways, to connect with yourself. You may not even realize how much you reflect the elements, both physically and metaphorically. Take out your magical journal and explore some of the ways the four main elements may show up in your life:

- Your inner earth—*Describe a time when you felt completely safe. | Describe a time when you felt utterly stuck.*

- Your inner fire—*Describe a time when you did something bold and brave. | Describe a time when you were so angry you saw red.*

- Your inner air—*Describe a time when you had an incredible breakthrough. | Describe a time when overthinking got the better of you.*

- Your inner water—*Describe a time when you were so happy you were driven to tears. | Describe a time when you felt like you were drowning in sadness.*

mother earth's help

Mother Earth doesn't just assist us with spells.

She wants to help us whenever she can, in whatever way she can, no matter who you are.

During my childhood, we had a family cat who would spend most of his days outside. There were plenty of nights when he never made it back home.

I would be sick to my stomach, imagining all the horrible things that could have happened to him—those worst-case scenarios that gnaw and gnaw. *What if he were lost at the other end of town? What if someone stole him? Even worse, what if he got run over by a car?*

Back then, I didn't practice magic like I do now, but as a born nature lover and then-vegetarian (vegan now!), I still held a deep reverence for Mother Earth. I felt our connection, even though I couldn't explain it and would've probably sounded ridiculous trying to.

I'm not sure how long he had been gone, but one time, in my desperation, I went out to our backyard and asked Mother Earth—more specifically, the trees—to safely bring him back home to me.

As if on cue, the wind rustled their leaves, and he came running through the gate, crying out for me as if I had called him.

For some unknown reason, this had worked, and it worked almost every time after that, too. I didn't dare question it; I just remained extremely grateful.

When you need some extra help from Mother Earth, all you have to do is ask. Do your best to be kind to her in return, even if that just means taking a few minutes out of your day to spend time in her presence.

grounding yourself

We, as humans, seem to have an endless list of demands and responsibilities, and because of that, our energy can sometimes get a little bit, uh . . . all over the place.

The way I see it, grounding is the act of energetically coming back home to yourself. The exercises below can help you become more present in your life as well as put you in the right headspace for spellwork.

Go outside—If you're lucky enough to have your own outdoor space available, go to it. If not, you can go to your favorite local park, beach, or trail—only with your caregiver's permission, of course! Take off your shoes and become reacquainted with the soil for a few minutes. Let Mother Earth's energy recalibrate you. (This is called *earthing*.)

Grow roots—Can't go outside for whatever reason? No problem. Go someplace quiet and close your eyes. Imagine roots growing from the soles of your feet, burrowing through the floor and foundation into the ground, planting you in place.

Do something mindful—Spend one-on-one time with your pet, relax in front of an open window, watch a nature video, hold your favorite plant/crystal, or drink a cup of herbal tea (spearmint is my fave).

Think about something that makes you feel a special connection to Mother Earth. It doesn't have to be super-magical; it can be something small, like walks around your neighborhood, or even just sitting underneath your favorite tree. What can you do to nurture this connection, to expand on it even more?

your witchcraft ethics

I can't tell you what kind of magic to make because I believe in the importance of free will, and it's *because* I believe in the importance of free will that I choose not to interfere with the free will of other people.

That means no love spells or curses.

You won't find either of those in this book, as most of them interfere with someone else's free will, which isn't nice.

As you'll probably notice, most of my spells and rituals have to do with things such as *self*-love, *self*-empowerment, *self*-worth, and bringing positive things into *my* life.

But cause and effect is a complex thing.

I recognize that it's possible that even those seemingly harmless spells could negatively impact others.

Remember when I said that witches have the magic within to bring anything we want into existence? That comes with a *lot* of responsibility. While I can't control every little thing that happens as a result of my spells, I still try my best to do no harm by practicing magic with integrity and minimizing damage wherever I see potential for it.

Before you cast a spell, carefully consider the potential ways your spell could affect you—positively *or* negatively. Are there any neutral ways it could affect you? How about the ways it could affect other people? If relevant, you might also consider how it might affect Mother Earth. (I recommend getting out your magical journal to make some good, old-fashioned lists!)

After you reach your conclusion, decide if the spell is really worth it. (Only *you* can do this.)

Now that you're almost ready to make some magic, what kind do you think you will make? In your magical journal, write a list of your witchcraft ethics with plenty of room for growth. Don't skip this part—it will be important soon!

before making magic

Before casting your very first spell, there are a few things I recommend doing first. (This applies to all future spellwork as well.)

Check in with your mind—If you're not thinking clearly, you may be more prone to forgetting steps or making mistakes. If you're feeling scattered, it might be a good idea to do a quick *grounding* exercise (see page 26).

Make a plan—Write down all the steps to your spell in your magical journal, even if you didn't create the spell. This will help you execute the spell in the way only you can. For example, with a prewritten spell, you may want to personalize the affirmation or switch out some of the tools. Leave room for notes after, too. These details show you what works for *you* and will help you with future spellwork.

Set the tone—Do what you need to do to create a private, distraction-free environment. Unless you have notes for your spellwork on your phone—or it's an important part of the spell itself—turn on *do not disturb* and stash it somewhere you can't get to it. Your notifications can wait!

Prepare your altar—The magical tools you'll be needing for your spell should all be within arm's reach. It's not the end of the world, but walking away from your altar to grab that "one more thing" three different times *might* eventually break the natural flow of your spell.

Give yourself some peace of mind—You may want to *cleanse* the area of any energy that doesn't match the magic you're trying to make. You can do this by simply lighting a white candle and letting that be that. If you want to further *protect* the area from any unwanted energy that might flow in and potentially mess with your spellwork, go ahead and place a black tourmaline crystal on your altar.

Make sure you're feeling your magic—Spellwork should never be daunting or stressful, and it certainly shouldn't feel like an obligation. If the idea of it doesn't make you feel happy or at the very least content, then walk away from your altar and come back later. Figure out what's not working, whether it's something personal or something about your spellwork that needs to change.

your first spell

Congratulations—you've made it, witch! Your very first spell is going to be all about the star of the show: you. The fact that you're deciding to go on this magical journey is kind of a big deal, so now you're officially going to give yourself permission to do so.

WHAT YOU'LL NEED:

A rose quartz crystal

Your list of magical ethics (see page 28)

DIRECTIONS:

Sit by your altar. Place your rose quartz crystal and your list of magical ethics in front of you. Begin by reading your list out loud, going point by point. Don't just say these statements—*feel* them becoming part of your being.

Next, hold the rose quartz crystal close to your heart and speak this affirmation: "I am allowed to be a witch. I am allowed to make my own magic, even if it doesn't look like anyone else's. I am allowed to make mistakes, and I am allowed to go easy on myself, for I am learning new things every day. Most of all, I am allowed to have fun on this journey."

Sit in silence with your rose quartz crystal for a few minutes. Close your eyes and imagine the kind of witch you'd most like to be. Go one step further and silently claim this witch as yourself, right now, in this very moment, not in some faraway and unknowable future.

When you're finished, say "So mote it be" to declare your spell as powerful and true.

Don't forget to write down the details of your spell! If anything unexpected happened, or you decided to do something differently at the last minute, make sure you take note of that.

feeling confident yet?

It's *totally* normal not to feel confident when you've just started something.

I mean, you probably wouldn't feel confident on the first day of learning a new topic at school, and starting your witchcraft journey is no different!

It may take a lot of time and practice to build up your self-esteem about magic. My advice? Read as many witchcraft books as you possibly can (don't stop after this one); don't be afraid to ask tough questions and dig to seek answers; then experiment, experiment, experiment until you find your groove.

You'll get there eventually.

Have a little patience with yourself.

Something that used to cause me a lot of anxiety (and honestly still does, but mostly on behalf of new witches) was seeing other witches say, "That's not how you do *xyz*! *This* is how you do *xyz*." But you know what I came to realize? "This" is usually just their own personal preference.

Not fact.

For example, some witches like to do their manifestation rituals on the full moon, whereas some witches, like me, prefer to do their manifestation rituals on the new moon (more on these practices a little later).

Who's wrong?

Nobody.

Make your own magic whenever and however it feels right to *you*!

when they're staring off into space
& unusually quiet,

you don't have to worry that
they're angry, sad, or annoyed.

they're just trying to listen
for the strings of their heartsong.

—*the most beautiful melody in the world.*

PART II

your intuition

"what's intuition?"

Has there ever been a time when you knew something without actually *knowing* it? A gut feeling you couldn't shake no matter how hard you tried, even though there was no "logical" reason behind it? Just an unexplainable knowing with no fear?

That right there is your *intuition*, witch, and it can show up as:

- Thinking about someone you know and getting a text/call from them a few minutes later.

- Canceling plans because something doesn't feel quite right, and later finding out that something less than ideal happened where you were supposed to be, like an accident or an argument.

- Buying a book because you can sense you're supposed to read it, and it changes your life.

- Circling an answer on a test not because you know it to be correct but because something in you told you it is. It ends up being right.

- Knowing that a friend hasn't been loyal to you even though there are no typical signs, and then something—or someone—confirms it for you.

And that's just the beginning.

Experiences like this show you that you know *way* more than you think you do.

They also show you how imperative it is to not only listen to yourself but wholeheartedly trust yourself.

While some of the intuitive hits you get might just be cool little reminders that your intuition is on point (like the anticipated text or call), much of the time, your intuition acts as your inner guide, pulling you toward what's good for you and pushing you away from what isn't.

We all have intuition, but sadly, not many people know how to tap into theirs or understand what it's trying to tell them, and it's no wonder—it isn't exactly a skill that's taught in school. We also live in a society where we're supposed to follow the rules, and intuition doesn't work like that.

Some witches practice something called divination to help them get more in touch with their inner wisdom, and that's something I'm going to teach you in this section!

Whenever you have an intuitive hunch in the future, keep track of it in your magical journal, even if it doesn't immediately appear to be "correct." It very well could come true later, and you'll definitely want to go back and see how right you were!

intuition game

Intuition games like this can exercise the accuracy of your hunches. Plus, they're a lot of fun!

WHAT YOU'LL NEED:

Scrap paper

A writing utensil

A medium to large jar with a lid

DIRECTIONS:

Begin by taking your scrap paper and tearing it into ten semi-equal pieces. On those pieces, draw any symbols you'd like. Some suggestions to get you started are a moon, a star, a sun, a flower, and a butterfly.

Fold those pieces of paper in half, and then in half again. Toss them into your jar. Put the lid on. Shake, shake, shake.

Next, take the lid off, then reach in and pick a random piece—don't open it right away, though! First, use your intuition to try to guess which symbol is on the paper, and *then* open it. This is a game, after all, so keep track of how many times you get it right!

> Pay attention to how it felt when you made the right guess—before you opened the paper and found out for certain. Chances are, that's how your intuition will feel when you're right about something in everyday life, which will make trusting yourself in those moments a whole lot easier!

"um, okay, but what's divination?"

Divination is the practice of using tools such as tarot cards, oracle cards, and pendulums to receive magical messages.

(Yes, crystal balls are sometimes used, too!)

Just like portrayals of witches are highly dramatized in media, portrayals of divination tend to be, too. No, it's not going to start storming the second you take out your box of tarot cards (though it would be cool if it did), and no, you're probably not going to predict someone's tragic and untimely death.

There *is* a small grain of truth to these depictions, though: depending on how you choose to use them, divination tools can give you a glimpse into your future.

Predicting stuff isn't the *only* thing they can do, however.

Most of the time, I like to use divination as a means of gaining deep, magical insight about my life and goals—to self-reflect on where I've been, to get clear on where exactly I am now in my journey, and to find some guidance about my path moving forward.

"wait. i thought you had to be psychic to use tarot cards & stuff?"

I can see why you would think that.

Growing up, my mom collected tarot cards and oracle cards filled with beautiful beings like angels and faeries. I loved to sit down and go through them, admiring the artwork and dreaming that I could one day be a card reader . . .

But that's as far as it went for many years.

I didn't even try to learn how to read them because I, like so many people, was under the impression that I had to have some innate psychic gift to understand their wisdom.

Eventually, I learned that just like anyone can be a witch, *anyone* can dabble in the art of divination if they want to, so now I do—every single day of my life. (Just to clarify: you do *not* have to be a witch in order to do divination, or vice versa. Anyone can. However, it's a very popular practice among today's witches.)

To read the cards, all you need is one thing: your intuition. As you know by now, this is something everyone has.

Some people might even say intuition *is* an innate psychic gift. (I'm some people.)

In my opinion, when you ask a question of your tarot cards (or your other divination tools), you're the one who actually provides the answer—anything they say comes right from within you. You may not *think* you know those things, but you do, even if it's deep, deep, deep down on a subconscious level. All your tools do is translate it in a way you can better understand.

telling the future

Before you even so much as think about touching a divination tool, it's important for you to understand something: nothing—and while we're at it, no *one*—can predict your future with complete and 100% certainty.

What divination tools *can* do is show you what there's potential for. *It's all about possibilities.*

Personally, I don't think my fate is set in stone. It's constantly being shaped by my thoughts, decisions, and actions; therefore, it's ever-changing. Divination tools can only predict so much based on what I'm thinking, deciding, and doing at this very moment.

And if I get an answer I don't like, I do whatever I can to change it, practically and/or magically.

Because like I said, I am never powerless.

I am power*ful*.

And so are you, witch.

Do you think you write your life story as you go, or do you think it was prewritten for you, and you're just living it out? Is it maybe a little bit of both?

your divination ethics

We've already talked about your ethics regarding your overall witchcraft practice. Now we're going to get specific and talk about your ethics regarding your divination practice.

I can't tell you what kind of witchcraft ethics to have, and I can't tell you what kind of divination ethics to have, either.

That's up to you, as it should be!

However, I will give you a little guidance, which you can either take or leave. I just ask that you stop and consider it carefully. Divination can be helpful and even fun at times, but it can also be very serious and should always be approached as such.

In this book, I'll be teaching you how to do divination for yourself and about yourself. (Others may be brought up in your readings, but I suggest you handle it in a noninvasive way.) Personally, I think that's the best place to start. If you're interested, you can do divination for other people once you get some practice in.

With that said, I do strongly caution you against doing readings about others unless they give you explicit permission to do so.

How would you feel if someone did a reading about your personal matters without telling you? Uncomfortable, I'm sure. Maybe even totally violated, depending on what type of information they are seeking. Keep that in mind and treat others the way you would want to be treated.

Finally, I strongly caution you against asking overly serious questions about others (and even yourself).

Just because you *can* ask certain things doesn't mean you *should*.

In your magical journal, write a list of your divination ethics. Make sure to tab it so you can go back to it whenever you need a reminder or to revise things you've changed your mind about.

tarot cards

There's some debate on where tarot originated, but most people believe it started as an Italian playing card game back in the 1400s, eventually transforming into the divination tool we all know and love today.

Cartomancy is the practice of using cards for divination.

When you think of tarot, the first thing you think of is probably the Rider-Waite-Smith tarot deck.

The Rider-Waite-Smith deck was first published in the early 1900s and is considered by many to be the traditional deck. It's also the most popular among witches and other tarot practitioners.

Because of the way tarot (and more specifically, the Rider-Waite-Smith deck) has been showcased in all forms of media—books, TV, movies, even music—most people are familiar with iconic cards such as Death, The Devil, and The Lovers, even if they don't know exactly what they mean.

tarot structure

Tarot has a structured seventy-eight-card system (it's not as scary as it sounds, I swear!), and some modern interpretations choose to include more cards. This system is split into two defined parts: the major arcana and the minor arcana.

The major arcana—Makes up the first twenty-two cards (#0–21). They tend to represent big themes in your life—think *major*, life-defining lessons, people, and events. These are the cards you want to pay the most attention to in a reading because they'll point toward anything super-pressing that might be affecting your life.

The minor arcana—Makes up the remaining fifty-six cards. Split into four suits (cups, pentacles, swords, and wands), these cards represent the *minor*, everyday things you might deal with. Each suit also contains a four-card court (page, knight, queen, and king), which can represent people/personalities (you or others) that may come into play. The minor arcana cards hold less weight than the major arcana cards, but small things have the potential to snowball into something huge, so do pay attention—you could easily avoid some drama!

tarot misconceptions

Tarot has had an undeniable impact on media and pop culture, yet most people only know a few surface-level things about it. Much of that knowledge is misinformation that scares them away from getting their own deck and learning how to use it.

So let's clear some things up:

- You do not have to be given your first tarot deck as a gift, and it's definitely not "bad luck" to buy your own. Unless the gifter knows you really well, I encourage you to do your own deck picking—that way, you can make sure you get one you really connect with!

- Tarot cards are symbolic in their meanings. If you pull The Devil, the literal devil isn't going to rise from the fiery pits of hell to get you. More likely, it points toward a toxic person (which can sometimes be you) or pattern present in your life.

- You're allowed to read for yourself; in fact, it's amazing practice for if/when you want to read for other people. Just try not to be too biased in your interpretations since the topic—*you*—is so personal! (It happens to the best of us.)

- You don't need to memorize the card meanings. There isn't going to be a quiz you either pass or fail. Just try to have a good grasp on the general vibe of the card so you have a starting point for your intuitive interpretations, even if that means consulting a guidebook here and there.

- There is no "right" way or "wrong" way to read the cards, so don't let anyone try to tell you otherwise. Everyone's intuition is going to interpret stuff differently. Your unique perspective is what makes your readings so special.

- You don't have to read using reversed cards (aka upside-down cards), but honestly, they aren't as bad as some people make them out to be. A lot of the time, they just show you something that you need to work on or overcome, which can be some pretty important information to know!

picking a tarot deck

Choosing a deck—let alone your first one—can be a stressful experience. There are already countless in existence, and there are more and more coming out every single year. How is a witch supposed to choose?!

Here are a few things for you to consider:

You may want to start with the traditional deck: the Rider-Waite-Smith. There are a few different versions to choose from, such as *Radiant Rider-Waite Tarot* or *Tarot Vintage*. Once you learn how to read with those cards, you can read most seventy-eight-card decks with ease.

Most decks you'll find are illustrated. Some are hyperrealistic, others are cartoonish, and some fall somewhere in between. Some are pastel; some are moody. Take time to think about what kind of art style you prefer.

Some decks feature people or animals. Some feature witches, goddesses, faeries, angels, dragons, or unicorns. Some feature crystals or plants or even characters from pop culture. The list goes on and on and on. Which theme do you think *you* would connect with the most?

You may come across a deck you feel an unexplainable pull toward, even though you don't necessarily connect with the art style or the theme. As always, trust your intuition—it's probably telling you that you'll connect with it in less obvious ways.

Once you land on a deck, you'll want to magically cleanse it with the usual tools we've already gone over (see pages 19–20), or you can just knock on the top of the deck three times. (Three is a super-magical number in witchcraft, so witches often do magical things in groups of three.)

the major arcana meanings

There are *many* ways to look at the cards. These are just my own personal distillations and are by no means intended as the be-all, end-all. There's a lot more to tarot meanings than you'll find in this book, but this is a great place to start if you're feeling overwhelmed. And if you are, I totally get it! Seventy-eight cards are a *lot* to take in. It took me years to become familiar with each and every one of them. I still struggle sometimes, especially with the court cards. (Ugh.)

When you pull a card, read it with your gut first. Take in the colors, the symbols, the animals, the people. What does it mean to *you*? Once you have that down, take a glimpse at my meaning and see if you can put your interpretation into that context.

If you can't, then stand by your intuitive interpretation. You hold all the knowledge, so you're probably trying to tell yourself something only you can "get."

The major arcana tells the story of the fool's journey (card 0). These cards reveal the big blessings, the almost-impossible challenges, and everything else we go through in life that shapes us, from beginning to end.

0: The Fool—You're taking the first step on a grand new adventure (upright). | You might be scared to start something; put fear aside and take the leap! (reversed)

1: The Magician—You're manifesting your dreams and goals (upright). | Your lack of self-belief is blocking your success (reversed).

2: The High Priestess—Your intuition is spot-on in this situation (upright). | You're ignoring your inner wisdom to your own disadvantage (reversed).

3: The Empress—You're flourishing in so many beautiful ways, especially creatively (upright). | You aren't nurturing yourself enough (reversed).

4: The Emperor—You've got everything under control (upright). | It's time to take back your power (reversed).

5: The Hierophant—You might find value in following tradition (upright). | Don't be afraid to do things your own way (reversed).

6: The Lovers—You have an important choice to make involving your personal desires (upright). | Your heart may be leading you astray (reversed).

7: The Chariot—Your determination is pulling you forward (upright). | Your lack of motivation is halting your progress (reversed).

8: Strength—You're strong enough to do anything (upright). | Don't doubt your inner strength so much (reversed).

9: The Hermit—Look within for guidance (upright). | You're spending a little too much time alone with your own thoughts (reversed).

10: Wheel of Fortune—You're having an amazing stroke of luck (upright). | Don't let bad luck get you down; it will all come back around (reversed).

11: Justice—You're being rewarded for sticking to your morals (upright). | You may need to face the consequences of your own actions (reversed).

12: The Hanged Man—You're resting between big chapters (upright). | Your impatience is making things so much worse than they need to be (reversed).

13: Death—This version of yourself is over and it's for the best (upright). | You're hanging on to an old version of yourself that no longer serves you (reversed).

14: Temperance—You're blissfully balanced (upright). | You need to create a little more harmony in your life (reversed).

15: The Devil—There's a toxic person or pattern in your life (upright). | Do something about that toxic person/pattern before the damage is done (reversed).

16: The Tower—Your life is going to be turned upside down (upright). | You're fighting necessary change and causing yourself more pain (reversed).

17: The Star—Your life is about to get *sooo* much better (upright). | Keep having faith and keep going (reversed).

18: The Moon—Something important is about to come to light (upright). | Despite your fears, it's okay to be exposed and vulnerable (reversed).

19: The Sun—You're about to have very good reason to be a happy-go-lucky witch (upright). | You're not letting yourself do what gives you joy (reversed).

20: Judgment—You're feeling called to step up and do something huge and unexpected (upright). | You're ignoring the call because you fail to see how amazing it'll be (reversed).

21: The World—You're celebrating a long-awaited accomplishment (upright). | You're afraid to move on to the next grand adventure, but there's nothing to fear (reversed).

the minor arcana
cups suit meanings

The first minor arcana suit we'll look at is the cups, which is associated with the element of water. These cards speak to your experiences with emotions, intuition, and inspiration. Many of them have to do with relationships, romantic or otherwise.

Ace of Cups—You're being blessed with a new feeling or connection that has potential to be expanded upon (upright). | Why aren't you doing anything to take this thing to the next level? (reversed)

Two of Cups—You can trust this deep, loving connection with someone (upright). | There may be a rough patch in a relationship, so give it some extra care (reversed).

Three of Cups—Your friend group is absolutely thriving (upright). | Oops—friendship fallout on the way! See if you can salvage the good (reversed).

Four of Cups—You're becoming bored with everyone and everything (upright). | Your inaction is officially negatively impacting your emotional well-being—change it up ASAP! (reversed)

Five of Cups—You're grieving and it's making you blind to your other blessings (upright). | It's *been* time to move on (reversed).

Six of Cups—You're feeling delightfully nostalgic (upright). | You need to realize that there's a difference between reminiscing and being stuck in the past (reversed).

Seven of Cups—You have so many options that speak to your heart (upright). | You're overwhelmed by the choices—pick what *feels* right! (reversed)

Eight of Cups—You're leaving something that no longer fulfills you (upright). | You refuse to walk away even though things probably won't change (reversed).

Nine of Cups—You have *so* much to be thankful for (upright). | You might be acting a little bit ungrateful (reversed).

Ten of Cups—You're living your happiest life (upright). | You're living the dream, but it doesn't really feel like it's enough anymore (reversed).

Page of Cups—The daydreamer who gets attached to a new fictional character every week (upright). | Someone who's a tad emotionally immature (reversed).

Knight of Cups—The charming and romantic type who follows their heart (upright). | A person who *seems* charming and romantic until you get to know the real them (reversed).

Queen of Cups—The typical empath who takes care of everyone (upright). | A people-pleaser who needs to focus on their own feelings for a change (reversed).

King of Cups—Someone who's balanced and mature (upright). | An emotionally manipulative person (reversed).

pentacles suit meanings

Next up is the pentacles suit, which is related to the element of earth. These cards have to do with things such as stability, nature, and prosperity. Love it or hate it (and there are plenty of reasons to hate it), the material world we live in has a constant impact on us!

Ace of Pentacles—You've been given a material opportunity with tons of potential (upright). | You were given that potential, only to throw it away (reversed).

Two of Pentacles—You're trying to balance school, life, and other responsibilities (upright). | You're not prioritizing the right stuff (reversed).

Three of Pentacles—You're working with and learning from others (upright). | You'll need to start playing nice with others in order to accomplish anything (reversed).

Four of Pentacles—You're feeling content with your resources, such as allowance or toys (upright). | You're afraid to use your resources in case you don't get more in the future (reversed).

Five of Pentacles—You might feel like you're missing out on something (upright). | You're being given a helping hand, so take it (reversed).

Six of Pentacles—You're giving (or receiving) a generous gift (upright). | You may experience a lack of charity (reversed).

Seven of Pentacles—You're growing something to see if/how it thrives (upright). | You haven't seen results yet and you're rightfully frustrated (reversed).

Eight of Pentacles—You've been working hard to make sure you achieve your goals (upright). | You're too caught up in the tiny details to get anything done (reversed).

Nine of Pentacles—You're a self-made success and you know it (upright). | You aren't enjoying your success enough (reversed).

Ten of Pentacles— You've reached your ultimate goal (upright). | You reached your ultimate goal but still don't feel satisfied—why? (reversed)

Page of Pentacles—A person who's figuring out their life and goals (upright). | Someone who has no direction or prospects (reversed).

Knight of Pentacles—Someone who makes smart, deliberate moves toward their goals (upright). | The one who's afraid to try new things and take healthy risks (reversed).

Queen of Pentacles—The one who flawlessly manages their schedule and everyone else's (upright). | Someone who's overworked and overburdened (reversed).

King of Pentacles—The one who makes sure everyone around them has what they need (upright). | Someone who's greedy (reversed).

swords suit meanings

Now for the swords suit. These cards represent the element of air. The themes of this suit are intellect, ideas, and communication. Some of the most "reality check" type cards appear here, which can be hard to face, but you know what? Sometimes those reality checks are *needed*.

Ace of Swords—You have an idea with tons of potential (upright). | You're deciding not to follow it through (reversed).

Two of Swords—You're making a choice between two directions (upright). | Stop pretending you don't know what you want to do (reversed).

Three of Swords—Your heart is broken (upright). | You've been focused on the rain clouds a little too long; time to get dry and move on (reversed).

Four of Swords—You need to rest your body and your mind (upright). | You refused to recharge, so your body and mind decided to take a break for you (reversed).

Five of Swords—You may have won the debate, but you lost a lot of respect in the process (upright). | Put aside your ego and fix what you broke (reversed).

Six of Swords—You're departing from a difficult situation to find healing (upright). | You're carrying too much baggage to properly move on (reversed).

Seven of Swords—You have to be clever to get what you deserve sometimes (upright). | Your actions might be a bit selfish (reversed).

Eight of Swords—You feel trapped (upright). | You're not as helpless as you claim to be (reversed).

Nine of Swords—You're very anxious about something (upright). | You've let your worries get the best of you (reversed).

Ten of Swords—You've been betrayed (upright). | Pick yourself back up and move on (reversed).

Page of Swords—That person who loves to learn and texts you a new fun fact every day (upright). | The type that would spread rumors or misinformation (reversed).

Knight of Swords—A person who isn't afraid to chase after their dreams (upright). | Someone who does things without thinking of the consequences (reversed).

Queen of Swords—Someone who isn't afraid to speak their truth (upright). | A person who cuts others down with their words (reversed).

King of Swords—The smartest person you know (upright). | Someone who doesn't take anyone's feelings into account when making decisions (reversed).

wands suit meanings

Finally, we have the wands suit! This suit is related to the element of fire. Here, you'll find cards that have to do with things like passion, creativity, and energy. (As a creative person, I find that the wands cards tend to show up for me a *lot*.)

Ace of Wands—You're having a burst of creativity with potential (upright). | You're not following where your passion is trying to lead you (reversed).

Two of Wands—you're putting some plans into motion (upright). | You're like, "I want to do the thing, but IDK where to start" (reversed).

Three of Wands—You're about to see the outcome of all your hard work (upright). | You're not seeing the results you expected by now—get back to the planning board! (reversed)

Four of Wands—You're feeling comfortable and at home with the people around you (upright). | You aren't feeling supported or understood (reversed).

Five of Wands—You're in an argument that's gotten too heated (upright). | This can't be solved until everyone calms down (reversed).

Six of Wands—You're finally getting the recognition you deserve (upright). | You shouldn't be scared to be the center of attention— you've earned it! (reversed)

Seven of Wands—You may have to defend yourself against people hoping for your downfall (upright). | You're letting your haters get to you too much (reversed).

Eight of Wands—You should expect some progress, like, now (upright). | You aren't happy with the speed of things (reversed).

Nine of Wands—You're still standing after an exhausting challenge (upright). | Don't give up yet, okay? (reversed)

Ten of Wands—You're taking on a lot, but you're almost done (upright). | You burned yourself out by carrying too much (reversed).

Page of Wands—That person who's passionate about something new every day (upright). | A person who can't find their passion in life (reversed).

Knight of Wands—Someone who charges toward every desire they have (upright). | The wild and reckless type (reversed).

Queen of Wands—That person who isn't afraid to shine brightly (upright). | Someone who needs to tap into their confidence (reversed).

King of Wands—The one who does what they love and empowers everyone else to do the same (upright). | A moody and angry person who scares others (reversed).

your first tarot reading

It's time to do your first reading! (You've got this!)

WHAT YOU'LL NEED:

A purple candle in a holder

An amethyst crystal

A lighter or match

Your deck

Your magical journal

A writing utensil

DIRECTIONS:

On your altar, arrange your purple candle and amethyst crystal however you'd like. As you light your candle, say, "I open myself to receive messages from my intuition. I trust my inner wisdom without fear or hesitation, for it would never tell me something I don't already know or can't handle."

Now, take your deck and shuffle it for a few moments, or until you're satisfied that the cards are mixed up enough.

It may feel a little silly, but I want you to introduce yourself to your deck and let it know that you're going to ask some questions. This is called a deck interview, which can be done before using any new deck you get.

For each of the three prompts below, hold your deck in between both hands and ask your question. Shuffle, then pull a card. (*Always* prompt your deck before pulling a card; otherwise, you'll just get a random message with no context, which is super-unhelpful.)

+ "Now that you know who I am, who are you? Describe yourself with one card."

+ "How can I best connect with you?"

+ "If you could give me any piece of advice right now, what would it be?"

As you move through each of these questions, make sure you write down the questions as well as your interpretations of the deck's answers in your magical journal. When you're finished with your reading, thank your deck for giving you its time and energy, then either let your candle burn down or extinguish it and use it for your next reading.

daily tarot practice

If you want to learn tarot, a great way to become familiar with the cards is to do a daily one-card pull. I like to go over to my altar after I wake up and pull one to help set the tone for my day.

You can ask whatever question you'd like, but here are some questions/prompts I have in my rotation:

"Which intention would best serve me?"

"What is the energy/theme of my day?"

"How can I kick butt and meet goals?"

Come back to your altar before you go to sleep and contemplate how this message played out. This way, over time, you'll learn what each card means for *you*, making your future readings that much more accurate!

Challenge: try pulling two cards to answer a single question/prompt, using your own common sense and intuitive creativity to combine their meanings. For example, let's say you pull The Tower and Nine of Cups for your intention. I'd interpret this as, *when it seems like everything is going awry, take a moment to remember how many blessings you still have left.*

tarot spread to remind you of your purpose

CARD 1

What is my purpose?

CARD 2

Which action can I take right now in order to live up to my fullest potential?

CARD 3

A message to empower me on my current path.

When you feel a little lost in life, do this three-card spread to help guide you out of the woods. Interpret each card individually and then see if you can find any connections across the cards—not just in their meanings, but in their illustrations and symbols. What do they tell you? Some symbols have common meanings, but your own personal associations are often much more powerful.

Have you ever thought about what your purpose could be? Is it different than the card you pulled? Keep in mind that you can have more than one. Also, your purpose might not be something obvious, like helping others *or* being a good friend. *Sometimes your purpose can be something simple such as* being happy, *which is just as valid.*

other ways to use tarot cards

Daily magic—For this, you're going to purposely pick a tarot card to represent the energy you want to embody that day. For example, if you want to have a relaxing and restful day off, try displaying the four of swords on your altar.

Journaling—Tarot cards can be used as journaling prompts, too. To do this, ask your deck to give you a random card, or, alternatively, you can purposely pick a card that you want to write about. Once you have your card, explore what it means to you and how it relates to your life or current situation. Is there any guidance you can take away from this card?

> Try pulling a tarot card to help inspire some passages in your magical journal, whether it's about a magical topic or a personal one.

Spellwork—I've been known to incorporate tarot cards into my spellwork. The way I see it, each card holds the energy of its unique meaning, and you can invite that energy into your spell in the same way you would with candles, herbs, and crystals.

tarot spell for self-confidence

This spell is perfect whenever you need a confidence boost, whether it's for a specific occasion (like giving a presentation, standing up to someone, or doing anything that scares you), or just in general!

WHAT YOU'LL NEED:
The Queen of Wands tarot card
A red candle in a holder
A lighter or match
A tiger's-eye crystal
Three cinnamon sticks

DIRECTIONS:

Hold your Queen of Wands card up to eye level and affirm, "This is who I am: a confident star." Place it down flat in the middle of the spellwork area on your altar.

On top of the card, place your red candle. As you light it, say, "I am confident and *strong*."

Placing the tiger's-eye crystal next to or in front of your candle, say, "I am confident, strong, and *courageous*."

Finally, take your three cinnamon sticks and creatively place them in/around the other components of your spell, such as bordering it in a triangle shape, if space allows. As you place your third and last cinnamon stick, say, "I am confident, strong, and courageous now and always. So mote it be."

Let your candle burn down or extinguish it and use it for a future confidence spell.

You may also choose to carry the crystal with you or make it into a bracelet/necklace so it can inspire confidence on the go!

oracle cards

One of the questions I'm asked most is: "Hey, amanda, what's the difference between tarot cards and oracle cards?"

The answer is *way* less complicated than you probably think.

By now, you already know that most tarot decks have a structured seventy-eight-card system based on the traditional Rider-Waite-Smith tarot deck. In other words, when you pick up any tarot deck, you pretty much know what you're going to get, adjusted for some artistic license.

That's not the case with oracle decks.

Each oracle deck in existence is unique. I can't give you meanings because those can only be found in each deck's individual guidebook.

I find that there's a difference in the type of messages you get from tarot cards versus oracle cards, too. Tarot decks tend to have more mundane and practical meanings (*not* a bad thing), whereas oracle decks usually speak more to your inner world—gentle guidance, thought-provoking messages, positive affirmations.

I use and love both kinds of decks, and I think there's room for both in a witch's life.

As with your first tarot deck, you'll want to search around until you find an oracle deck you connect with. You'll also want to write about why you chose it, cleanse it, and conduct a deck interview with it (see pages 54–55—yep, same questions and everything). Since oracle card meanings tend to be less direct, you might have to be a little creative with your interpretations!

oracle spread to check in with yourself

Just like you check in on the people in your life, you should take the time to check in on yourself, too. In case no one has ever told you this before: *your well-being is just as important as the well-being of those you love.* With that said, let's see how you've been and how you can better take care of yourself moving forward with this simple three-card spread.

CARD 1	CARD 2	CARD 3
The part of myself I've been prioritizing lately.	The part of myself I've been neglecting.	The best way to show the neglected part of myself more love.

daily oracle card affirmation ritual

When you get a new oracle deck, you'll want to pull a card every day until you're familiar with them all. This is *especially* important since every oracle deck is different and will ultimately give you a totally new experience. You may find that you form a stronger relationship with the cards using this hands-on daily affirmation ritual.

WHAT YOU'LL NEED:

An oracle deck
Your magical journal
A writing utensil
A piece of scrap paper

DIRECTIONS:

Shuffle your oracle deck while asking the question, "Which affirmation would be most helpful to me today?"

Once you have your card, I want you to display it on your magical altar and really take in the illustration as well as the guidebook meaning. What energy does this card give off? What intuitive messages do you get when you look at it? Be sure to write down any words or phrases that come to mind in your magical journal.

Next, I want you to use those notes to craft a sentence-long affirmation.

If you don't know what to write, start with the phrase "I am _____" and fill in the blank. For example, "I am worthy of all the things I want," "I am shining my light for everyone to see," or "I am willing to practice forgiveness for my own peace of mind."

Once you have your final affirmation, write it down on a piece of scrap paper and find a place to display it on your altar, preferably next to your oracle card pull.

Repeat this affirmation aloud to yourself and say, "So mote it be."

Come back to your altar at least two more times that day and repeat this affirmation to yourself so you won't forget it. If that's not possible because of school or activities, you can also take a picture of it and set it as the lock screen on your phone.

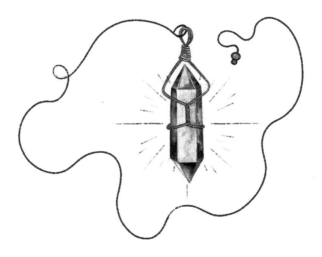

pendulums

Before you know what they are, pendulums can seem pretty unassuming. After all, they usually resemble necklaces: a long chain with some sort of charm at the end.

In fact, some witches—like me—take off their necklace and use it as a pendulum in a pinch. (What can I say? Convenience is *everything*.)

Most people would probably be surprised to learn that pendulum dowsing—aka using a pendulum for divination—is not only an ancient practice but a very powerful divination method, as the answers you'll receive are very straightforward.

Using a pendulum is effortless. You just have to ask a question and wait for the pendulum to swing this way or that. Which answer will it be: "yes," "no," or "maybe"?

Whichever answer you get, it will be certain to confirm your inner wisdom.

picking a pendulum

Like I said, pendulums are usually long chains with charms at the end. The charm can be made from any number of materials, such as wood, metal, or resin. You can even find acorn or seashell pendulums.

Most commonly, though, it will be a crystal.

For divination purposes, I highly recommend you get your hands on an amethyst pendulum, as it has properties that help support your intuition.

However, *any* crystal you vibe with will likely make for a good one.

I'm sure you already know this by now, but the first thing you should do when you get your pendulum is cleanse it. After, take out your magical journal and write about why you picked it, then get ready to do the pendulum version of a deck interview, which I'll guide you through next!

Don't have access to a pendulum? Use a necklace with a pendant or even a string with a paperclip tied to the end instead.

your first pendulum session

Okay, now that you have your pendulum, you're probably eager to use it!

WHAT YOU'LL NEED:

A clear quartz crystal

Your pendulum

Your magical journal

A writing utensil

DIRECTIONS:

First, place your clear quartz crystal down on your altar while saying this affirmation: "I offer myself clear and enlightening answers during this pendulum session."

Sit in such a way that you can comfortably rest your elbow on your altar because your forearm needs to be raised and steady. Next, using your dominant hand, pinch the charmless end of your pendulum chain between your index finger and thumb. Let any leftover chain rest between your other fingers and palm. The charmed end should dangle freely.

Now you're going to program your pendulum.

This is where you teach your pendulum which way to swing to indicate "yes," "no," and "maybe." Go through each one, doing the motion you prefer to represent each answer. Choose whatever makes the most sense to you.

Here's what I do: a clockwise circle for "yes," a counterclockwise circle for "no," and a horizontal sway for "maybe."

After you program it, test it. Ask some yes or no questions you already know the answers to, like:
"Is my name _____?"
"Am I __ years old?" or
"Do I live in (town/state/country)?"
(Switch it up and ask questions you know to be false, too, so you can fully test its accuracy.)

The movements may take a while to start, or they might only be slight, so pay close attention!

Take note of everything that happens in your magical journal. Don't become too disheartened if your pendulum doesn't seem to be working correctly, or if it gives confusing or contradictory answers. Sometimes you just have to work with it a little more so it can become attuned to your energy and intuition.

now what?

There are so many ways you can work with your pendulum on the regular, but here are a few you might like to try!

Double-check yourself—Sometimes we get intuitive tugs, but we aren't fully confident in the way we interpret them. When in doubt, pull out your trusty pendulum and ask it if you're interpreting things correctly, making sure you voice your interpretation clearly. If you get a "no," then ask your pendulum follow-up questions until you get to the bottom of it.

Tarot/oracle card readings—I absolutely love to use my pendulum in my tarot and oracle card readings. As I interpret each card, I ask my pendulum if I'm on the right track. If I get a "yes," then yay, but if I get a "no," then I know I need to spend a little more time tuning into my unique intuition, even if it means straying from the usual card meaning.

Make decisions—Within *reason*, of course. You should never do something risky just because your pendulum told you to (or your tarot and oracle cards, for that matter). Always use a combination of intuition and logic just to be safe. You can start by using your pendulum to help you with small decisions. For example, you can pull out your pendulum to help you decide what to have for breakfast or to pick out what to wear. Go through each option and ask, "Should I have/wear _____?" until you get a "yes." Works like a charm every time.

other divination methods

Maybe you can't get your hands on a deck or a pendulum, or maybe you just don't vibe with them. Don't sweat it. Here are some divination methods that use tools that are easier to come by, and one that doesn't require tools at all.

Bibliomancy—This is divination using books. Pick a book, ask a question, close your eyes, and flip to a random page. With your eyes still closed, point to a random part of the page. Open your eyes. That's your answer. Sometimes it will be nonsensical or even silly—it's okay to laugh!

Cloud gazing—You don't need anything for this except yourself and a cloud-filled sky. Find a place to lie on the ground, ask your question, and see which shapes the clouds take on. What do these symbols mean to you, and more importantly, how can they answer your question? Let your imagination and intuition run wild!

Shufflemancy—I saved the best for last, because in my opinion, this one is the most fun! This is divination using music. All you have to do is get a playlist ready, ask a question, then press shuffle. See which song plays and listen carefully to the lyrics. The answer might surprise you or even move you.

More divination methods you can look into as you grow your practice: numerology, Norse runes (aka the Elder Futhark), Celtic Ogham, tasseography (aka tea leaf reading), palmistry (aka palm reading), and scrying.

every time you see me,
i'll be a different person,
but that doesn't mean
i'm faking anything.

i'm just leaving a welcome mat out
for every version of myself.

i'm entertaining the beauty
of my own comings & goings—
no matter how permanent,
no matter how temporary.

i've never felt more real in my life.

—*you should try it sometime.*

PART III

your cycles

"cycles?"

Yes, cycles!

By definition, cycles are things that happen again and again and again with a definitive beginning and end. There are *so* many cycles you experience on the regular that you might not even be consciously aware of.

Whether that means the weekly cycle, the moon cycle, or the seasonal holiday cycle, every one of these cycles has a magical energy that affects us and the world around us.

In this section, I'll be teaching you how you can live your life and work your magic going by some of those cycles present in your life.

In my opinion, I think it's always best to work *with* that existing energy instead of trying to work *against* it.

Make no mistake, though—you can make whatever kind of magic you want to make whenever you want to make it! You know how I feel about rules in witchcraft: generally speaking, do whatever the *hex* you want. Your witchy intuition should always come first.

However, I *do* find that certain magical acts are more powerful during certain days, moon cycles, and seasonal holidays.

I would venture to say that most experienced witches do, too, even if we don't always agree on what's most powerful and when. (These are, as always, my own takes, based on my own personal experiences as a witch.)

When it comes down to it, why *not* take advantage of these cycles whenever you possibly can?

the weekly cycle

Let's start with your day-to-day.

Each day of the week is associated with a celestial body—mostly planets, as well as the sun and the moon—which gives it an overall energy that is favorable to certain spellwork and other magical doings:

Sunday (*The Sun*)—This day is often associated with rest in our society, but it's actually a great day to do workings that speak to your power and success. There's a lot of happy energy on this day, too, so let loose and do whatever brings a smile to your face.

Monday (*The Moon*)—Usually recognized as the beginning of the work/school week and therefore the go-get-'em day, nonmagically speaking; magically, it's best to take it slow and tap into your intuition. Meditation, divination, and dream-related workings are best performed on this day.

Tuesday (*Mars*)—This is a much more intense weekday. There's a "fired up" energy that comes along with it, so do workings that require or relate to empowerment, bravery, and strength. Follow your passion and confidently create something you love.

Wednesday (*Mercury*)—There's already a lot of weird energy surrounding this day because it's so in-between. It's not at the beginning of the week, but it's not at the end of the week, either. Do something unexpected and outside of the box. Express yourself and your magic in new ways.

Thursday (*Jupiter*)—Prosperity and abundance are the themes of this day. Take this time to recognize your self-worth. Strive for the things you know you deserve and believe you can achieve them.

Friday (*Venus*)—It's all about self-love on this day, so take extra special care of yourself and do nonstressful spells that honor *you*. It's also a day for beauty and friendship, so why not get dressed up and spend some time with the people you care about the most?

Saturday (*Saturn*)—The first day of the weekend is typically considered a time for play. Magically, it's a day more suited to buckling down and getting super-serious. Set boundaries—magical or otherwise—and do some deep and meaningful self-reflection called *shadow work*.

As you align your magic with the days of the week, you'll find what works for you. If your intuition tells you to cast a prosperity spell on a Tuesday afternoon, even though Thursdays are considered best for that, go ahead and do it anyway. Maybe there's something about Tuesday's energy that works better for *you*.

sunday

nurturing your inner child

We all have an inner child: a version of yourself that just wants to play, giggle, and make backyard mudpies—those were always fun, weren't they?

As we grow up, sometimes the activities we did when we were really little are considered *immature* or *childish*, so in order to fit in, we may stop doing them, even if we still enjoy them. Sunday asks you to rethink this and do whatever makes you smile.

If you'd like, you can play a game of tag. You can run through the sprinkler with friends. You can even make finger paintings—solo or with a friend or family member.

And remember: carry this energy with you every day, not just on Sunday.

spell for success

What better way to begin your week than with an easy, breezy spell that sets you up for the best week possible?

WHAT YOU'LL NEED:

A piece of scrap paper

A writing utensil

The sun

DIRECTIONS:

On your piece of scrap paper, write down one thing you want to achieve this week, making sure to word it as an affirmation: "This week, I am super-successful at _____."

It can be a specific goal you have—like starting or finishing a creative project—or something simple like "finding joy in the little things."

Afterward, leave this piece of scrap paper on a windowsill the sun reaches, or somewhere outside in direct sunlight. Remember to repeat your affirmation as you set it down, followed by, "So mote it be."

That's pretty much it!

Feel free to leave it there until the sun goes down.

You see, the sun—which Sunday is named after—is already known for energizing things, and it can certainly energize your goals, too.

If it's cloudy outside, no worries. The sun is too powerful to be totally cast out; it's always somewhere just beyond the clouds. Your spell will still work fine. Alternatively, you could place your affirmation underneath the sun tarot card or a citrine crystal (associated with sun energy), and that would work just as well. It's all about that symbolism, witch.

monday

practicing meditation

In my nonexpert opinion, meditation is one of the most important things you can do for your overall well-being, as it has the power to reduce stress, balance moods, and promote peaceful sleep (because I've always struggled to sleep, it's been life-changing for me).

Many of us have also found that going within and finding stillness can help you connect with the voice of your intuition.

There are just *so* many benefits!

If you haven't meditated before, you might think it's just sitting down, closing your eyes, and wiping your mind free of thoughts—it's no wonder that sounds boring and even impossible to most people. While that's sort of a type of meditation, it's far from the only one.

Anything that brings you into present awareness can be meditation; for that reason, it's also a great grounding technique.

I do a three- or five-minute meditation every morning. That's all you really need—just a few spare minutes. You don't have to meditate every single day if you don't want to. Add it to your Monday routine at first and see what it brings to your life as well as your magical journey.

A typical meditation would be to go to a quiet place, sit comfortably, set an alarm for your desired amount of time, and close your eyes (or at least soften your focus) until your alarm goes off. During your meditation, try not to spend too much energy fighting your thoughts—just accept that they're going to happen and pay them as little mind as possible (some days will be easier than others). Let go and just *be* for a few minutes.

If this doesn't work for you, however, there are countless ways to meditate:

Take a walk—Put away the headphones and concentrate instead on the sounds of nature, people, and life. Simply be aware. See what you notice. (This might be hard to achieve the first few times; just do your best.)

Look at a tarot/oracle card—Pick your favorite card and display it at eye level. Gaze upon it and try not to fixate too much on any one detail as you consider what it means. You can play soft instrumental music in the background to help you relax.

Work with water—Monday is associated with the moon, which is associated with water because it tugs at the tides. Find a body of water like a lake, a river, or an ocean and focus your attention on it. Raindrops also work. If none of this is doable, you can fill something like a bathtub, bowl, or cup.

spell bag for serene dreams

Spell bags are my favorite because they're like crockpot recipes—just throw the spell ingredients into the bag and let it work its magic!

This one is great if you want to increase the intuitive messages you receive in your dreams.

WHAT YOU'LL NEED:

A small drawstring pouch

Dried lavender buds

Dried rosebuds/rose petals (for beauty rest . . . get it?)

Amethyst crystal chips

DIRECTIONS:

As you add each ingredient into your bag, remember to say a positive affirmation, like, "I sleep soundly every single night. My intuition speaks to me loud and clear through my dreams. I always wake up feeling well-rested." You get the gist. Tailor it however you need.

When you're done, say, "So mote it be," and then go place it underneath your pillow, or tuck it inside of your pillowcase. (I highly recommend the latter in case it breaks open while you're fast asleep!)

Make sure you cleanse your spell bag every Monday to keep its energy fresh. If I forget to do this, I find that my sleep becomes more restless, or I may see an increase in nightmares.

Whenever you have a dream, make it a habit to write it down. Even the silliest and most nonsensical dreams can have an underlying intuitive message that can be useful for your waking life. What happened from beginning to end? Was anyone else in your dream, and did they say anything? What symbolism did you notice, if any, and what does it mean to you?

tuesday

reigniting your passion

Between long hours at school, spending time with family and friends, and (perhaps) involvement in extracurricular activities, who has the time or energy to find something to be *passionate* about?

Not many.

The idea of carving time out for yourself might not only seem impossible or impractical, but it might even give you feelings of guilt. I, too, have had thoughts like, "but I could be giving my time to someone else!" and "I could be doing something productive instead."

You *have* to take the time to find something you're passionate about and do it, even if it's just for an hour or so every Tuesday, because you're worthy of having so much *more*.

When I was a little girl, I spent a lot of my time playing computer games, as they were a much-needed escape.

I've had people ask me why I don't become a gaming streamer. Truth is, I want games to be the one thing that remains sacred to me, the one thing I do that's just for my enjoyment and no one else's. I don't want it to become a stressor or an obligation. I deserve that one thing, and so do you. Your passion is part of your magic, even if you don't share it with anyone else. It's magic for no other reason than it lights you up.

What's your passion? If you're not sure, what do you think it could be? Maybe it's something you've always liked but haven't had a chance to dive into, something mentioned somewhere in this book, like tarot or crystals, or something interesting someone mentioned to you in passing. Go ahead and see that curiosity through.

spell to spark change

May this spell light a fire in you to help spark fierce change in our world.

WHAT YOU'LL NEED:
Your magical journal
A writing utensil
Your phone
Powdered cinnamon
An orange candle in a holder
A lighter or match

DIRECTIONS:

First, you'll have to pick a political or societal topic you're passionate about, such as health care, book banning, climate change, or systemic racism. What change is it that you would like to see?

Take out your magical journal and write it at the top of a fresh page, followed by an affirmation: "I am able to help make this change happen. I put in all of the necessary work. I do not give up until I see justice."

Next, you're going to write a list of things you can personally do to make this change.

This can mean protesting, signing petitions, making donations, or something else entirely. Nothing—as long as it's *something*—is too little to make a difference. Depending on the issue, you may need to do some research to see which course of action would be best, and this can also be part of doing the work.

First, take a picture of your list so you have a clean version to refer to later, and then take the paper out of your journal. Now sprinkle a tiny pinch of cinnamon on the paper to give yourself the energy needed to go through with this plan. Fold the paper in half twice (keeping the cinnamon inside) and place your orange candle on top of it. As you light the candle, don't forget to say, "So mote it be."

wednesday

using your voice

Wednesday is the day of communication. To recognize your magic is to recognize the power of your words, so when someone hurts you, let them know. When someone interrupts you, keep talking until you say everything you need to say. Most importantly, tell your story with honesty and inspire others to do the same. If you need some assistance, light a blue candle, carry an aquamarine crystal, or display the Queen of Swords tarot card on your altar.

spell to challenge yourself

People are often afraid of switching things up and doing something a little different, even if they want to. That's because it can mean taking a risk, like looking silly or embarrassing themselves. But if you don't take a chance and do it, how will you ever know? Even if it doesn't go the way you wanted, at least you'll figure out whether it's for you. Go ahead and cast this spell to help push you out of your comfort zone!

WHAT YOU'LL NEED:
Your magical journal
A writing utensil
Scrap paper
A small to medium bowl
A rainbow moonstone crystal

DIRECTIONS:

In your magical journal, write a list of five to ten things you can do to switch things up. Think of things you want to do but have been putting off out of fear. Perhaps it's something small and subtle like "wearing my hair in a new style," or big and scary like "trying out for the school play."

Prepare as many pieces of scrap paper as you need. Write down each point from your list, each on its own paper. When you're done, fold each piece of paper in half twice.

Next, take all your folded pieces of paper and deposit them in the bowl. Create a hollow space in the middle of the bowl and place the rainbow moonstone crystal there.

Pick a paper out of the bowl. Commit to doing whatever it tells you to do by turning it into an affirmation: "Today, I welcome the new experience of _____ and everything that it has to teach me. So mote it be." Carry the crystal with you so it can energetically support you. Cleanse it and return it to your bowl when you're done. Pull out a new piece of paper every Wednesday; the more chances you take, the easier it'll become!

thursday

knowing your worth

No matter who you may be, and no matter what may have happened to you in the past, you very much deserve to have and experience wonderful things. Pay close attention to this on Thursdays, and don't you dare settle for less than what you know you deserve—not from others, and certainly not from yourself.

You *are* important, so start acting like it, witch!

spell jar for prosperity

This spell jar is to help you attract more prosperity into your life. Remember, prosperity comes in forms other than money or material objects such as toys, so be on the lookout because you may receive it in unexpected ways. For example, you might suddenly find yourself rich in things like awesome friendships or joyous experiences!

WHAT YOU'LL NEED:

A medium jar with a lid

Dried peppermint leaves

Dried chamomile flowers

A citrine crystal

Three coins of your choice

DIRECTIONS:

Fill your jar with your dried peppermint leaves and dried chamomile flowers, making sure to leave plenty of empty space at the top—this is the "base" of your spell jar, so to speak.

Next, arrange your citrine crystal and three coins on top of your herb base. When you're pleased with how it looks, put the lid on your jar.

Hold the jar in your hands and say this affirmation: "Prosperity is growing and flourishing in my life. I am abundant in all things amazing. I am worthy of all the blessings being bestowed upon me. So mote it be."

Keep your spell jar on your altar however long you'd like. I like to keep one there permanently, refreshing the herbs every few weeks or months, usually on a Thursday.

It's important to know that your spell jar won't do all the work for you. You'll need to actively put yourself in situations to increase your chances of receiving prosperity, like talking to your classmates or peers (to increase the chances of gaining awesome friends) or, with your caregiver's permission, leaving your house more (to increase the chances of joyous experiences). As you do these things, you may find that you attract more.

friday

being a better friend to yourself

Friday is a day dedicated in part to friendship.

Confession: I've never had a lot of friends.

I was a painfully shy child and a very socially awkward teenager, so it was difficult for me to make them.

I still have visions of myself sitting alone at a long, empty lunch table for years on end. (What I wouldn't give to go back in time and give that child a *huge* hug . . .)

Eventually, I became so desperate for friends that I clung to the few I *did* have for as long as I possibly could, even if they weren't very nice to me.

I wish I hadn't done that, but I know better now.

Sometimes we're so busy trying to be good friends to other people that we forget that we need to be a good friend to ourselves, too.

Part of being a good friend to yourself is letting go of people who are no longer good for you and trusting that better people will come along.

I'll admit that I still have some trouble doing this, especially if that person has been in my life for a long time.

Letting go of people doesn't mean that you have to cut them off and shut them out (though that can be necessary at times). Sometimes it just means creating a little distance—loving those people from afar, no matter how hard it is, so you can finally focus on and love *yourself* better.

spell for magical self-love

Acts of self-love are healing for the heart. *Magical* acts of self-love take that one step further.

WHAT YOU'LL NEED:

Pink Himalayan salt
A small bowl
A rose quartz crystal
A pink amethyst crystal
A rosewater face mask (optional)
Your magical journal
A writing utensil

DIRECTIONS:

First things first: pour pink Himalayan salt into a small bowl to gently cleanse away any energy that's not aligned with self-love and place it somewhere on your altar.

Now, to invite in energy that *is* aligned with self-love, place a rose quartz crystal beside the bowl on one side and a pink amethyst crystal on the other. (You can just use two rose quartz crystals or one rose quartz + one purple amethyst crystal if you don't have pink amethyst, which is a little harder to come by.)

If you have a rosewater face mask, apply it as directed. Remember to remove it whenever the package recommends.

Next, get out your magical journal and list at least three things that you love about yourself (if you can keep going, then definitely do so). This can include your physical appearance, but don't stop there. There is so much more to you, like your personality, accomplishments, and skills.

Perhaps you love your brown eyes, how empathetic you are, or the way you never give up in the face of adversity.

Once you're finished with your list, I want you to tenderly place your hand over your heart while you read this list aloud, signing off with, as always, "So mote it be." Challenge: try to list new things you love about yourself during each magical Friday self-love session!

saturday

doing shadow work

Shadow work is a phrase you'll see a lot of in witchcraft spaces . . . but what does that term actually *mean*?

For me, it's about going within and facing the things I keep hidden in my shadows—painful memories, past mistakes, truths that bring me feelings of shame. These things can be easier to ignore than to deal with, so I hide them not just from others but from myself.

Shadow work is about bringing those things into the light so that I can work through them and/or integrate them into my "everyday" self.

I dissect painful memories to see how I'm allowing them to negatively impact all areas of my life.

I own up to my mistakes and appreciate how they've helped me become the person I am today.

I face the truth of who I am, even if it's not always pretty, even if it makes me less "perfect" to myself and/or others.

But that's just the beginning—to do the actual *act* of shadow work, I create a safe and protected space for myself, pick a topic, and journal my every thought. I like to think that I'm writing my way through acceptance and healing.

Here's how:

Try freewriting to do your Saturday shadow work. *Which shadows have been following you?* Pick up your pen and spill your thoughts and feelings for ten to fifteen minutes (be sure to set a timer)—you'll be surprised how much you have to say!

You can use your tarot/oracle cards as a guide through your shadow work, too:

CARD 1	CARD 2	CARD 3
Something about myself that I hide out of fear or shame.	Why I hide it.	What good would come from accepting this part of myself?

Asking yourself these questions may bring up some tough emotions. If you feel overwhelmed, please don't hesitate to call a trusted friend or family member, or seek professional guidance in whatever way it's available to you.

spell to strengthen your boundaries

I don't know about you, but I give away so much of my energy to others, like agreeing to conversations, activities, or favors I don't have the bandwidth for. This can happen with friends, family, peers—*anyone*. Sometimes we just want to make sure the people in our lives are happy and taken care of, even if it drains us and makes *us* unhappy. That's never okay. This spell can help you strengthen your boundaries before the new week.

WHAT YOU'LL NEED:
Four black tourmaline crystals

DIRECTIONS:

Sit on the floor in front of your altar and place the four black tourmaline crystals on the floor in the space surrounding your body: one in front of you, one to your left, one to your right, and one behind you. (This effectively creates a protective "boundary" around you. Make sure you give yourself plenty of space in case you want to stretch out and stay for a while.)

As you place each crystal, repeat these affirmations:

- ◆ "I am no longer willing to give more of myself than I want to or am able to."

- ◆ "I only say 'yes' to the things I want to do."

- ◆ "I allow myself to say 'no' to things that don't excite me without feelings of guilt."

- ◆ "These boundaries are nonnegotiable, and I make sure they're respected by myself and others."

Stay in this space and contemplate your boundaries for a few minutes. Before you get up, make sure you say, "So mote it be." You *might* want to do this spell every Saturday to help you recover from a long week of giving your energy away.

the moon cycle

The moon cycle lasts approximately thirty days from beginning to end. During this time, you may find that the magical energy around you and within you shifts and changes as well. (After all, the moon controls the tides, and we know from science class that we're mostly made up of water, so it makes total sense that it would affect us so much.)

While there are technically eight moon phases total because the waxing and waning phases are split into several smaller stages, we're going to stick with the four main phases to keep it nice and simple for now.

Go ahead and look up the dates of the phases in the coming days. Mark them in your calendar and try making magic with the moon, beginning with the new moon and going through the waning moon, if possible. See what works for you and tweak what doesn't.

New moon—This is the first phase of the moon cycle. When the moon becomes completely dark, it brings the energy of new beginnings into every area of your life. Manifestation spells and rituals are *very* commonly performed during this phase.

Waxing moon—As the moon grows in size, prepare to get busy and take action toward your goals so they can come into fruition during the full moon.

Full moon—Celebrate your accomplishments! Full moon = full power, so do any spell you'd like. This is also an excellent time for releasing rituals; as the moon comes full circle, so do many things in your life, so say farewell to anything you don't need anymore.

Waning moon—As the moon wanes—or begins to disappear—you should wane, too. I'm *not* saying that you should literally disappear (you shouldn't), but you may want to take a breather from all the work and celebrating you did during the waxing and full moon phases. Self-reflect and show gratitude for the journey you just had before a new cycle starts.

*Tonight, go outside (or to a window) and gaze up at the moon.
Silently take note of the phase as well as how you're feeling, not just
physically but emotionally. Do you think this could possibly be
correlated to the moon phase? Why or why not?*

new moon

starting over

It's never too late to start over.

You don't have to maintain friendships that don't make sense for you anymore.

You don't have to keep reading the same kind of books, listening to the same kind of music, or eating the same kind of food.

We can get stuck in our ways when we're used to doing and being certain things, but the truth is that you don't have to be the same person you were yesterday. You can just decide to be different one day—to follow a new routine, to have new goals, to go in an unexpected direction.

That's not to say that starting over will be easy. In many ways, it won't be. There were times I decided to enact major changes to make my life more authentically mine, only to be met with negative reactions from the people around me.

For example, when I decided to call myself a witch, I did lose a friend or two who clearly disapproved (though they would never admit it).

Some people don't like change, but they *especially* don't like it when the people close to them start to change. Perhaps it's because they feel like they're being left behind (even though they aren't).

The new moon gives you an exciting blank slate to work with, so make the most of it and ignore anyone who wants less for you.

Perhaps you should take this time to connect with people who are more aligned with who you are now and who you want to become.

manifestation

To manifest is to "magic up" your desires, to make them a reality. That's what you've done for all of your spells so far, but new moon manifestation spells and rituals are special because you can magic up a whole list of things that don't necessarily have to do with one another—almost like your own magical wish list!

WHAT YOU'LL NEED:
Your magical journal
A writing utensil
Bay leaves
A Sharpie
A cauldron or bowl

DIRECTIONS:

First, start by *thinking* of things you would like to manifest. This isn't something that should be rushed, so you might want to take a few days to really ponder it. Ask yourself, "What does my ideal life look like?" Then go from there. Try not to set limits on yourself.

Now make a list in your magical journal. Write "So mote it be" at the bottom to finalize it.

Get your bay leaves and Sharpie. On each bay leaf, write one of your manifestations. (You can write a few keywords if they're too long to fit!)

Start to transfer the bay leaves into your cauldron. As you do, imagine each one burning up, sending your manifestations out into the world via the fire energy in your mind, and then turning to ash. (Even though there isn't any real fire involved, visualizations of fire can be a super-powerful thing.)

Keep the cauldron filled with bay leaves on your altar however long you'd like. When you're ready, dispose of the bay leaves however you wish, such as burying them in your garden or backyard.

when your manifestations don't come true

Oh no—you manifested something, but it's been a while and nothing's happened!

This is a scenario every witch has experienced.

Here are a few things to consider:

Give it a moment—Not all magic is instantaneous. Some things take time. Are you being impatient? If you can, try to take your mind off it. Have you heard the phrase "a watched pot never boils"? Obsessing over it won't help your case!

You may not be ready yet—I know this might be frustrating to hear, especially because you *feel* ready, but sometimes a manifestation won't find you until it's time.

It actually did manifest—Sometimes our manifestations come true, and we don't even realize it because there's a disconnect between expectations and reality. If you aren't specific enough with what you manifest into your life, the way it comes true may be more small-scale than you wanted, or maybe just different and disappointing. Try again next new moon.

Something better is brewing—Maybe you didn't dream big enough (that's why you should never sell yourself short), or maybe the dream you had isn't the best thing for you when it comes down to it. Be open to the possibilities—you might be in for some amazing surprises!

Real-world barriers—I would be remiss not to mention that systems of oppression such as racism, sexism, classism, homophobia, and fatphobia are built to keep some people down while building others up. These things could affect your manifestations/spellwork. It can be exhausting to deal with these obstacles, but try to keep your chin up and don't be too hard on yourself. You are *not* a weak witch; society is just in need of significant change.

waxing moon

making moves

All my life I've been an avid reader.

Eventually I started to have dreams about being a writer myself.

I wrote a few poems here and there and even the occasional short story. I wanted so badly to write a full-length book of my own, but I wasn't very consistent with it. It usually began with a burst of inspiration and *sometimes* a few written pages before it fizzled out.

My follow-through? Pretty bad.

If only I had opened my eyes and realized that my dreams wouldn't become reality unless I actually did something about them.

Here's the thing.

If you want your manifestations/spells to come true, your efforts can't stop after you say, "So mote it be." In my experience, things *will* sometimes drop into your lap, but most of the time, the magic will happen because you continue to speak words and take actions that align with your desires, especially during the waxing moon.

I know that I never would have become an author if I didn't stop telling myself, "I can't do this" or "it's too difficult," if I didn't push myself to put pen to paper and keep going until I scribbled the words "the end."

I find that we procrastinate about the things that are important to us because we're afraid of getting them wrong. It's okay to be afraid, but take that fear and use it as fuel to lead you through it. Maybe it'll be a disaster, or maybe it'll be wonderful. You won't find out till you try, will you?

Some of you might be asking, "If I have to do so much work, what's the point of casting spells?"

Think of it like this: the spell gives you a metaphorical set of wings. It's up to you whether you actually take flight.

spell for motivation

You may not always feel like putting in work toward your manifestations, even during the waxing moon. I totally get it. Whether you need to start a new task, continue one, or finish one, it can be intimidating. Cast this quick little spell whenever you need to get motivated to check something off your to-do list.

WHAT YOU'LL NEED:

A piece of scrap paper

A writing utensil

A small bowl

Coffee beans

DIRECTIONS:

On your piece of scrap paper, write down the immediate goal that you need motivation to accomplish.

Next, go ahead and place the bowl on your altar. Alternatively, you may also use a lid to a jar, or even a condiment bowl, if you happen to have one on hand.

Pour your coffee beans (you can also use coffee grounds) inside of the bowl, filling it up about halfway. You know how adults drink coffee for energy and motivation in the morning? We can use it in our spells for the same thing!

On top of your bed of coffee beans, place your scrap paper. As you sprinkle a few more coffee beans on top of the paper, repeat the following affirmation: "I am motivated to complete this goal of _____. I know how to get things done. Nothing and no one can stop me, including myself. So mote it be."

All done!

This spell is only designed for one goal at a time, but you can do it as often as you wish—even multiple times a day with different goals. The best part is that it will likely only take a few minutes of your time.

full moon

celebrating yourself

You should always take time to pause and celebrate your achievements, no matter how big or small. Don't blow past anything as though it's insignificant. If you do, you're going to feel empty later on when you look back and realize that you once dreamed of being exactly where you are now, yet you didn't stop to appreciate the journey it took to get there.

(I'm trying to be better about doing this, I swear!)

No, you don't have to throw an entire party every time you get an A+ on a paper, win a game, or have one of your manifestations come true. It doesn't have to be that dramatic.

Celebrating can mean *so* many different things.

Celebrating can mean eating dinner outside so you can watch the sunset.

Celebrating can mean going down to your favorite bakery and getting a little treat for yourself. (I may or may not do this regularly.)

Celebrating can mean stopping to give yourself a silent but heartfelt "congratulations."

When witches talk about full moon rituals, they're usually talking about releasing rituals. However, I think we should also normalize self-celebration as a ritual, even if it doesn't involve a spell. Celebrate what deserves celebrating, *then* get rid of what no longer serves.

releasing

Yay, your first full moon releasing spell will soon be underway! Get ready to energetically release anything you don't want to bring with you into the next moon cycle. This makes room for new manifestations to come your way.

WHAT YOU'LL NEED:

Scrap paper

A writing utensil

A garbage can

DIRECTIONS:

Tear your scrap paper into pieces big enough to write on. On each piece, write down one of the things you'd like to release. Keywords work, too.

Here comes the fun part.

When you're finished, take those pieces of scrap paper and rip them into teeny tiny bits. As you tear up each one, say, "I hereby release _____ from my life." Say "So mote it be," after the last one.

Where do we throw all the expired things we no longer want?

Right into the trash.

Yep, trash can be magical, too.

Go ahead and throw all those little bits of paper into your nearest garbage can. Make sure you take the bag out on trash day so you can get it as far away from your person as possible.

Feels good, doesn't it?

making moon water

You can make moon water during *any* moon phase, depending on what kind of magic you want to do with it, but the full moon = full power, so it's the most favorable time. Whatever intention you give it will be potent.

To make moon water, fill an airtight container with tap water. Whisper an affirmation into it, then close it. Leave the container under the full moon (or in a window), which will magically supercharge it. You can also surround the container with crystals, herbs, or cards that correspond with your intention. Just make sure you go out and grab it before the sun comes out!

How to use your moon water:

Drink it—Sip on it as it is or use it to make tea, lemonade, or hot cocoa. As you drink the liquid, you will also "drink" its magical energy.

Cleanse with it—Wash your face/hands with it or pour some into a bath to cleanse yourself. You can cleanse your water-safe magical tools with it as well.

Bless with it—Moon water is basically a witch's holy water, so you can use it to magically "bless" yourself, your tools, or anything else you'd like, as long as the object is water-safe.

waning moon

getting rest

When you're laser-focused on your goals and manifestations all the time, you can forget to stop and smell the lavender.

You might neglect to nurture your mind, body, and soul altogether by getting less sleep, abandoning any number of your interests and hobbies, or forgoing time with loved ones.

Luckily, the waning moon is a nice little pause before the next moon cycle.

During the waning moon, take out your calendar and do some serious reassessing. I bet there's at least *one* thing each week until the new moon that can be put on the back burner, or one thing so unnecessarily draining that it can be taken off the calendar altogether.

Once you free up some time for yourself, I want you to sit and do nothing, or at least something pleasant that doesn't require too much of your energy. Catch up on a TV show that you like or hang out with a low-maintenance friend who's okay with doing something a little more chill and laid-back for the day.

I do this thing where even when I'm supposedly resting, I eventually start thinking about all the things I have to do when my time is up. It can tie my stomach into knots and make me super-anxious. There have been instances where I've even stopped "resting" so I could begin that work and make those feelings go away.

That is *not* actually resting, and I know I'm far from the only one who has these tendencies.

Neglecting to properly recharge between the chapters of your life will inevitably lead to some major burnout, and that's not something you can feasibly work through (at least not well). This could delay progress on your end, so do future-you a major favor and rest during the waning moon so you can go into the next moon cycle more refreshed than ever before!

spell for gratitude

When was the last time you counted your blessings? Some believe that when you show gratitude, you're energetically calling in more things to be grateful for. Through the duration of the moon cycle (from the last new moon until now), keep track of all your joyful moments by taking photos and videos on your phone. (Tip: make albums to organize them by moon cycle.) They'll be important for this waning moon spell.

WHAT YOU'LL NEED:
A silver candle in a holder
A lighter or match
Your phone
Your magical journal
A writing utensil

DIRECTIONS:

Light your silver candle and say, "My self-reflection brightens my perspective."

Take out your phone and go through your moon cycle photos/videos, but don't flip through them like it's an old, dusty photo album your Aunt Mildred gave you to look at. Pore over each one slowly. Take the time to really *remember* what it was like to be in that moment. Explore every tiny, microscopic detail—how it felt, how it smelled, how it sounded. Shamelessly relive your happiness so you can more effectively write about it.

Now take out your magical journal. At the top of the page, write, "For all of the following things I am incredibly grateful, and I welcome more like them into my life." Use your photos/videos to guide you through making your list, but feel free to include anything else that comes to mind. End with "So mote it be."

Let the candle burn down or extinguish it and use it for your next gratitude spell.

the seasonal holiday cycle

Aka the Wheel of the Year, a set of eight pagan festivals that honor the seasons.

By celebrating these holidays, you may find that you're much more in tune with yourself, as the seasons often reflect what's going on in our own lives at the same time.

Most of these holidays are on different days every year, so look them up before you mark them down on your calendar. You can even buy a witchy calendar with the dates already incorporated. Most will also include the moon phases.

The approximate dates below are for the *northern hemisphere*. (For the southern hemisphere, look to the opposite side of the wheel for the correct holiday.)

Yule (*Winter Solstice*)—Celebrated on or around December 21, this is the shortest day and the longest night of the year. Witches will often decorate holiday trees, light yule logs, and share the joy of the sunlight's approaching return by giving and receiving gifts. The cold and darkness also give you the opportunity to look within, do some soul-searching, and tap into your resilience.

Imbolg/Imbolc—The midway point between Yule and Ostara is celebrated on or around February 1. The short, cold winter days are finally becoming a little longer and a little sunnier. Spring is starting to feel like it's within reach. As the earth thaws, so will you, so make way for new happiness and new growth by doing a bit of spring cleaning—both literally and magically!

Ostara (*Spring Equinox*)—This celebration of an equally long day and night is observed on or around March 21. Sunlight continues to be more present throughout our days, which is something to celebrate—go on and have a nice outdoor lunch or host an Ostara egg hunt. Allow yourself to indulge in some chocolate bunnies while you're at it. Nurture all the ways you've been growing.

Bealtaine/Beltane—The midway point between Ostara and Litha is usually celebrated on or around May 1. Sunlight is now becoming plentiful and the earth is finally awakening. Hints of summertime are heavy in the air. Consider donning a flower crown and having a bonfire, or do something else that speaks to your wild side. This is often a day for love, so be sure to let your family and friends know how you feel about them.

Litha (*Summer Solstice*)—Usually celebrated on or around June 21, this
   is the longest day and the shortest night of the year—that means the
   sun is now shining in full force! Celebrate the return of the light as
   well as all the things you have to be happy about. Partake in summer
   activities like throwing a barbeque or swimming. Don't be afraid to
   shine and have confidence in who you are.

Lúnasa/Lughnasadh—The midway point between Litha and Mabon is
   usually celebrated on or around August 1. Summer is beginning to slip
   away, and you may begin to see some small signs of autumn. This is
   the first of the three harvest holidays, commonly observed by baking
   or eating bread and picking sunflowers. It's also a time to review your
   yearly growth.

Mabon (*Autumn Equinox*)—Our second celebration of equal day and night is usually observed on or around September 21. Afterward, the nights will become longer and longer. In honor of the second harvest holiday, grab a pumpkin spice–themed treat and go pick some apples and pumpkins. Play in the vibrant leaves that are just beginning to fall. While you're at it, fall for *yourself*.

Samhain—The midway point between Mabon and Yule is usually celebrated on or around October 31. Autumn is departing; like it or not, winter is creeping in through the open door. The days are becoming very short, leaving little sunlight. As this is the final harvest holiday, this is a great time to honor the past year, as well as your past in general, including your deceased loved ones and ancestors.

> As the Wheel of the Year turns, you can add seasonal decorations to your altar (e.g., small holiday trees for Yule or autumn leaf garlands for Mabon), switching them out for the next holiday. Think of it as another way to honor Mother Earth's magic.

yule

soul-searching

If Yule has the least sunlight of the entire year, then why is it such a merry day? Why is it lovingly referred to as "Witchmas"?

Well, Yule is essentially the darkest point before the dawn. After Yule, sunlight will (very) slowly start returning to us—that's what we're ultimately celebrating, but that's not *all* we're celebrating. We're also celebrating the promise that our daily lives are about to change for the better.

Soon, we'll get to stop being so cooped up in our houses to protect ourselves from the frigid cold.

Soon, we'll get to go back outside and connect with Mother Earth— bask in the glorious warmth and vitamin D we've missed so much.

Soon, we'll get to feel a little more like ourselves again.

Those are all fantastic things to look forward to; however, once the holiday trees come down, the Yule logs get extinguished, and the gifts get put away, there will still be plenty of cold, dark days left. It's still winter, after all.

Depending on where you live, you'll have to deal with these things for at least a few more months, so why not go ahead and settle into the darkness? Put on an oversized sweater. Get yourself a cup of something warm and comforting so you can slow down and become better acquainted with one another.

The darkness is something to celebrate, too.

It's in our darkest hours—while everything is still and quiet—when we can finally turn within and explore our inner worlds, just like the seeds do in the ground before sprouting in the spring.

spell for resilience

Perhaps you feel like you need a *little* more strength than usual to get through winter. While it's my second favorite season after autumn, even I can get restless near the end, when those cold days do nothing but drag and drag and drag. Here's a spell you can cast around Yule—or at any time during winter, really—to help you build your resilience. You're going to make it through this season just fine, lovely!

WHAT YOU'LL NEED:
A gold candle in a holder
A small to medium tray
Evergreen needles
A lighter or match

DIRECTIONS:

Place your gold candle in the middle of your tray.

Sprinkle evergreen needles in a circle around the candle. (You can also use rosemary as a more practical option!)

As you light your gold candle, say the following affirmation: "I do make it through these remaining winter days. I am as resilient as an entire forest of evergreen trees. No amount of cold—or even an avalanche of snow—can topple me. So mote it be."

If you have the time, I recommend that you hang out and let your candle burn all the way down. As you do, imagine the flame and the evergreen (energetically) working together to help strengthen your resilience.

imbolg

emerging from your cocoon

By the time Imbolg rolls around, the signs of winter are beginning to fade. The air should be starting to warm up and the snow should be starting to melt, getting ready for new growth. You may start to see signs of spring soon, like birdsong and small patches of flowers in your yard.

Snowdrop flowers bursting through melting snow is my absolute favorite Imbolg imagery.

Maybe it's just the sensitive poet in me, but here's how I see it: When it's finally time for the snowdrops to be reborn, they take the name of the thing that prevented them from growing in the first place. They don't forget the lessons they learned from the frost while hiding deep within the cold soil; they let them become part of them, strengthen them.

When you finally emerge from your cardigan cocoon, remember what it was like to brave the cold. That version of yourself is what will help carry you into spring. You're so close now.

While the earth is getting ready for new growth, get ready to make some physical space for *your* next evolution.

This can include doing things like cleaning your room (or your altar) like you normally would, and/or doing the magical space cleansing on the next page.

home cleansing

There are many ways to magically cleanse your space, like with a cleansing water bowl spell. Below is a version you can do on/around Imbolg.

WHAT YOU'LL NEED:
A small to medium bowl
Tap water
Dried rosemary sprigs
Dried lavender buds
A spoon

DIRECTIONS:

Fill your bowl about halfway with tap water.

Add your rosemary sprigs (for cleansing) followed by your lavender buds (for a dash of spring; many witches use it for cleansing as well) to the water.

With your spoon, stir the water in a counterclockwise motion and say, "I hereby cleanse this home of winter's cold, icy energy. May it leave space for spring's warmth and rejuvenation in its wake. So mote it be."

Place the bowl on a flat and stable surface in your room/space—like your altar or an end table—so it can energetically cast out any negative, unwanted, or stale energy. (Make sure it's out of reach of small children and pets!)

Drain the water from the bowl and toss the herbs after a few hours.

In magic, a *clockwise* motion manifests/creates; a *counterclockwise* motion releases/banishes.

everyday ways to cleanse your space

While Imbolg is a great time to magically cleanse your room/space, it shouldn't be the *only* time you do so. Personally, I try to do some kind of home cleansing every full moon—sometimes every other—since it's a good time to banish any negative energy that might be stuck around in my space.

Use sound—Begin ringing your bell and, as you keep ringing, walk counterclockwise (starting at each door/threshold) through your space, letting the sound cleanse all that bad stuff away. This is one of the most basic space cleansing methods there is, so I think every witch should try it at least once.

Sweep—Witches can't actually fly on brooms, but one thing we *can* do is magically cleanse with them. For this, I recommend buying or making a special broom known as a *besom*. After you've swept with your regular broom, walk counterclockwise around your room/space, using your special broom to sweep the air—or the energy—just above the floor. Open your door and sweep it out.

Do a more everyday cleansing water bowl spell—For this, I would use rosemary (which cleanses), lemon slices (which purify), and whole cloves (which protect against negative energy). You can follow the directions for the Imbolg water cleansing bowl, subbing out these ingredients for the ones used in those instructions.

ostara

spell to nurture your growth

As the flowers have bloomed, so have you. But flowers don't just grow and stay vibrant forever. You have to keep nurturing them with things like sunlight and water throughout the season. Some say kind words of encouragement help them prosper as well. The same goes for you. Do this spell to nurture your own growth on Ostara.

WHAT YOU'LL NEED:

A small to medium basket or bowl

Green ribbon

A piece of scrap paper

A writing utensil

Three fillable plastic eggs

A chocolate bunny

DIRECTIONS:

Place your basket (or bowl) on your altar.

Inside your basket, place your green ribbon (green yarn or Easter grass—preferably the biodegradable kind—work, too) so it covers the bottom. This is meant to represent grass and Mother Earth's nurturing embrace.

Tear your scrap paper into three medium pieces. On each one, write one positive way you've grown as a person since winter.

These will need to be things you'd like to keep nurturing so they can continue going strong. They can include small new habits like waking up a little earlier to get ready for school, or a challenge with a specific end goal in mind, like committing to reading a certain number of books before the end of the year.

Slip each piece of paper into an egg of its own. As you do, repeat an encouraging affirmation, like, "I am fully capable of sustaining my new routine."

Close your eggs and put them in your basket. As you add your chocolate bunny (or a chocolate bar, if need be) to the basket, say, "So mote it be." (Chocolate is comforting; here, it symbolically nurtures your growth. Feel free to eat it after you're done!)

bealtaine

do no harm but take no negativity

Being human is complicated. We are never just one thing all the time—some parts of us can be gentle and vulnerable, like wildflowers; other parts can be fierce and devastating, like wildfires.

Around Bealtaine, you'll notice that sunlight and greenery are continuing to grow in abundance, and the summer heat is starting to cling to your skin. Like many witches, you can celebrate by putting on a flower crown and having a bonfire, with your caregiver's assistance. Use this time to think about and honor every aspect of yourself—your gentle along with your fierce.

This seems like a good time to talk about the concept of "do no harm but take no negativity" that is common among modern witches.

I actually *really* love this idea.

In my practice (and life), this looks like never intentionally doing harm to another person (my gentle side) while also never standing by and letting any harm come to me at the hands of another (my fierce side).

There are many ways to interpret and apply the phrase "take no negativity." Here are some simple but still-effective methods you can use:

Moving along—If a troll happens across your path, or if someone starts issues for the sake of it and can't be reasoned with, mute or block them (literally or figuratively). Just walk away, and make sure you tell an adult what happened.

Standing up for yourself—Is someone gossiping about you or trying to hurt your character? Okay, you can't just stand by and let that happen. Call them out on their nonsense.

Sending them love—Counteracting people's bad behavior with kindness often takes them aback and makes them reevaluate what they are doing. (Plus, the look on their face is usually *priceless*.)

spell jar to let loose your wild

One theme associated with Bealtaine is your *wild*—who you are without
the influence of people's judgments. These are things you might hide,
dampen, or change because they're not accepted by your peers or society.
Connect with the authentic and down-to-earth version of yourself with the
help of this spell jar.

WHAT YOU'LL NEED:

"Wild" things from nature (keep reading!)
A medium to large jar with a lid

DIRECTIONS:

Before your spell, go outside and collect some "wild" things—anything you
like that you would happen across in nature, such as moss, flowers, clovers,
tree bark, and rocks/pebbles.

Just don't pick anything you can't identify because it could be dangerous
(ask an adult for help with this if you're not sure), and don't go around
picking flowers from other people's gardens or defacing trees for their bark
(find fallen bark or even small twigs instead). Be mindful and respectful.

When you get back to your altar to do your spell, layer the items inside
your jar however you would like. For each of the items you put in it, take a
moment to envision something you want to do to let loose your wild.

Perhaps you want to stop wearing gender-conforming clothing. Perhaps
you want to embrace your body hair. Perhaps you want to go back to
laughing loudly and freely after other people have criticized you for it for
years. (Can you tell this one was a *little* bit personal?)

Once you're finished, put the lid on your jar.

Hold the jar in your hands and repeat the words, "I am my wild and my wild is me. From this point forward, I vow to be nothing other than my pure, beautiful, and unrestrained self for all to see."

As you say, "So mote it be," take the lid off the jar to energetically symbolize "letting loose" your wild.

Keep this jar on your altar for as long as you want, composting/tossing the ingredients when you're done.

litha

appreciating your sunny days

It's Litha. It's finally hot enough for people to be walking around wearing tank tops, shorts, and their cutest pair of sandals. The sun is shining brightly up in the sky; in fact, this day contains more sunlight hours than any other day of the year. By the time you go to bed, the sun may only just be *starting* to set.

This is a long and cheerful day—one made for barbeques, backyard swimming, boardwalk adventures, water parks, and beach days.

No matter what you choose to do, take advantage of the light while it's here.

It won't be like this forever, you know.

After today is over, the sun will gradually set earlier and earlier, and the air will eventually become cooler and cooler.

Of course, you still have *plenty* of time to enjoy nature and explore countless amazing summer experiences, but doesn't it seem like time passes the quickest when you're having the most fun? (Maybe that's just me . . .)

What I love most about Litha is how it teaches us a lesson that goes far beyond the season.

Appreciate the sunny days in your life because you never know what could happen. Tomorrow, the sky could open up and unleash an unexpected and devastating storm over you. While you're huddled in your shelter waiting for it to pass, you'll have all of those good times to hold on to.

They'll also remind you that you have plenty more to look forward to once it's all over.

The wheel of your life will *always* turn back in your favor again.

spell to reaffirm your worthiness

At the beginning of summer, you might hear people talk about doing things to obtain the "perfect summer body." This spell is about challenging that toxic idea and accepting that you're already worthy of having an amazing summer exactly the way you are.

WHAT YOU'LL NEED:
A full-length mirror

DIRECTIONS:

On a day when you're going to go outside and have fun in the summer sun, find a full-length mirror.

As you look at your reflection, I want you to pretend as though you're looking at your best friend, because that's exactly what you're going to treat yourself like.

And what do best friends do? Hype each other up!

If you haven't already, go ahead and give yourself a warm and welcoming smile.

Look yourself in the eye as you shower yourself with compliments along the lines of "OMG, you look absolutely incredible!" and "That top looks super-cute on you, witch."

Now, talk back to your reflection, agree with them, and say, "So mote it be."

Although this may seem like an overly simple spell, I think choosing to unconditionally love and accept your body in a society that's constantly telling you what's wrong with it is *extremely* powerful magic.

lúnasa

beginning your harvest

Lúnasa is the first of three harvest holidays.

In my area, this is when people start harvesting—or picking—ripe peaches and nectarines. Wheat is also harvested, which is then used to make bread, so witches refer to this as the "bread holiday" (which is adorable).

It's common to celebrate this harvesting of food; after all, it nurtures our bodies and gives us the energy we need to live our lives. That's certainly something we should all show appreciation for, witch or not.

I think it's also important to celebrate another type of harvest, too. Your own personal harvest.

At this point, you're nearing the end of the year. It will be Samhain before you know it. You've undoubtedly done a lot so far, so make sure you take a moment to think about all the progress you've made toward your personal goals. Harvest all of your wins and successes by taking special note of them. Pat yourself on the back for a job well done—you deserve it!

At the same time, start thinking about the things in your life that have been positive forces but have grown as much as they possibly can.

What needs to be harvested and enjoyed one last time—for now *or* for good—so you can continue to expand in new ways?

For example, I took guitar lessons when I was younger, and while I liked some aspects of it, it stopped inspiring me after a few years. I decided to stop taking lessons, which gave me the space to explore things I enjoyed a lot more. I began writing in this new spare time, which changed my life and eventually became my career.

I knew I was ready for a new adventure, and I'm so glad I listened to myself.

Perhaps you're ready for a new adventure in some area of your life, too!

spell to treat yourself

You deserve to treat yourself after everything you've put effort into this year. This spell helps you celebrate that and acts as fertilizer for future endeavors. Since this is the beginning of the harvest season—a very food-centric time— why not do a spell that incorporates some easy kitchen magic?

WHAT YOU'LL NEED:
A butter knife
Sunflower butter
A piece of bread
A plate
Sunflowers and a vase with water (optional)

DIRECTIONS:

Use the butter knife to spread sunflower butter onto the bread. Serve yourself with a nice plate. (It's a special occasion!)

If you have sunflowers, trim their stems (you might want to ask a caregiver for help with this) and stick them in a vase with water. Place them wherever you're choosing to eat, whether it's at a table or at your altar. Artificial sunflowers are fine, too.

Why all the sunflowers, you ask?

Sunflowers are harvested at this time, and they're also associated with happiness and good luck. You deserve both of those things and more, especially as you head into the remainder of the harvest season.

There's still plenty of time for you to do and harvest so many amazing things.

As you eat your bread, think ahead to everything you would like to harvest— or accomplish—before the end of the season.

Before you take the final bite of your bread, say, "I have already accomplished so much this year and only continue to do so. I am now accomplishing all of these things and more: (here's where you list them off!). So mote it be." Encouragement goes a long way!

Clean up and display the sunflowers on your altar.

mabon

drinking pumpkin spice for protection

We continue the harvest season with our second harvest holiday, Mabon.

The air is crisping up, making your nose turn red. You look up to see trees filled with brilliantly changing yellow, red, and orange leaves. People everywhere are wearing scarves and picking pumpkins. You might suddenly get inspired to bake an apple pie.

This is thought of as the Witch's Thanksgiving, so continue taking stock of your personal harvest and showing gratitude for yourself.

If you share this day with anyone else, make sure you express gratitude for them as well! You're amazing on your own, but there are surely those who bring value to your life, too, and they deserve to feel appreciated.

Around this time, people start drinking pumpkin spice–flavored drinks, including hot chocolate and milkshakes. Everyone seems just a *little* bit happier than they were before—oh, the undeniable magic of pumpkin spice!

No, but really—did you know that pumpkin spice actually has a *ton* of magical properties? It's especially awesome for prosperity, confidence, and protection workings.

Self-protection is vital, especially now, as you're harvesting some of your most impressive and long-awaited accomplishments. Not everyone will look on with awe and pride; some will look on with envy and jealousy, and that bad energy—intentional or not—could cause you to stumble.

Every time you drink your pumpkin spice beverage, make sure you whisper an affirmation of protection into it first. Just in case.

everyday methods for self-protection

Here are a few more ideas for protecting your energy, especially when it's not pumpkin spice season.

Moisturize—Take your preferred lotion and dab it on your finger. Using your lotion, create pentacle shapes on your skin, then rub it in like normal. This will create an invisible protective barrier for the day.

Enchant your jewelry—Take any piece of jewelry (e.g., a necklace, ring, or bracelet) and lay it in a dish filled with rosemary for at least a few hours. This will charge it with protective energy. When you're ready, put it on and find peace of mind knowing you're safe.

Imagine it—Close your eyes and picture a solid light in the color of your choice enveloping and protecting your body.

You should eventually get to a place where you're implementing protection every day—not just before spellwork, but before you do *anything!* (The same goes for cleansing and grounding. Try a routine of cleansing, grounding, and protecting yourself upon waking up.)

spell to fall for yourself

As the leaves fall, why not do a spell to help *you* fall for yourself?

WHAT YOU'LL NEED:
Your magical journal
A writing utensil
A piece of scrap paper
Three autumn leaves
Tape
A small to medium tray
Acorns or other signs of autumn (optional)

DIRECTIONS:

Make a list of reasons you're worthy of falling for in your magical journal. Avoid your physical attributes as much as possible; instead, describe your *spirit*. Are you a loyal friend? Are you exceptionally trustworthy or helpful? Go with things like that!

When you're done with your list, pick three of your favorite reasons. Tear up your scrap paper and write one reason on each piece.

Next, you're going to tape your papers to your autumn leaves—one reason per leaf. They'll be flatter and easier to work with if you have pressed them between the pages of a large book for a few days beforehand.

If you don't have autumn leaves where you live, then any naturally fallen leaf will do. Alternatively, you can buy artificial autumn leaves from the craft store or draw and color some autumn leaves and cut them out.

Lay your leaves in the middle of your tray, pausing to say each reason aloud using this format: "I am worth falling for because _____." After you say your last reason, say, "Therefore, like these leaves, I choose to fall for myself each and every day. So mote it be."

119

If you want to add an extra touch of magic, you can surround your leaves with other signs of autumn like fallen acorns, chestnuts, or maple seeds (those fun helicopter things).

Leave the tray on your altar for as long as you'd like; this past fall, I kept it set up for a few weeks because it was almost like fall altar decor and it made me happy to look at it every day.

samhain

honoring your past

Samhain is the overwhelming favorite Wheel of the Year holiday among witches—and that includes me!

Some witches even deem it so important that they refer to it as the Witch's New Year.

I can see why. It's the one day of the year when everyone's celebrating magic, as Samhain is usually observed on or around Halloween. (Yes, our beloved Halloween evolved from none other than Samhain!)

This is also the only day of the year you can dress up as witchily as possible and no one will even give you strange looks for it. Not that being a witch means you have to dress up any certain way—you don't—but it's much easier to wear a witch hat, for example, when so many nonwitches are walking around wearing them, too.

As it's yet another harvest holiday, it makes sense for you to continue thinking about all the things you've harvested this year. (Doing this while eating your Halloween candy—aka your physical "harvest"—wouldn't be totally off-theme, either!)

Since this is also the *last* harvest holiday, it means saying goodbye to this yearly cycle. As you do, make sure you also give a special thank-you to this year's version of yourself that will soon, too, be in the past—*forever*.

We move on so fast that we can forget entire periods of our lives. I look back sometimes and realize how many years are just . . . gone. I couldn't tell you a single thing that happened—not one memory, not one feeling, not one experience. It's like opening up a book and starting to read it from the middle.

What a shame it is to forget who I've been before, the phases of my life that made my existence possible today—this is why it's so important that you journal, not just to keep track of your spellwork, but to keep track of who you are and where you've been. Remember *all* of your magic, not just the intentionally witchy kind.

spell to honor your dead

Another way to honor your past is to honor your loved ones who are no longer on this earth. The veil between our world and the spirit world is said to be its thinnest on Samhain; therefore, many witches choose to invite their deceased loved ones to a silent supper. Let's start small by having a snack with them!

WHAT YOU'LL NEED:
A black candle in a holder
A lighter or match
A snack (I recommend something with rosemary, as it represents remembrance)
Photos or mementos of your loved ones

DIRECTIONS:

Before you begin, light your black candle to make sure your space is nice and protected from unwanted or negative energies. (This is important whenever you're doing spirit-related work, especially on a night like Samhain, when so many are roaming about. I don't say this to scare you; I say this to make sure you do what you need to do to keep yourself safe!)

Prepare your snack—a portion of which will be for your loved one(s)—and bring it over to your altar/table. Out of respect, make sure you place their portion down first, as you would for a guest.

Next, arrange their pictures or mementos by their place setting. Make it clear who it's for by saying, "Name(s), I would love if you enjoyed a little snack with me."

As you eat, have a moment of silence for their lives. Look at their photos/mementos and reminisce. In your mind, catch them up on whatever they may have missed since they've been gone. Tell them how much you love them and miss them. (I truly believe they're able to hear your thoughts, or at the very least feel the energy you're sending their way.)

When you're done, say, "Thank you for coming. May your memory always be clear in my heart. So mote it be." Blow out your candle. Feel free to eat their snack once they've left—they won't mind!

everyday ways to connect with your dead

I connect with my deceased loved ones and ancestors on a daily basis.
I believe it helps my loved ones live on and stay part of my life, and by
connecting with all those who came before me (aka my ancestors), I
can learn from them and get a better idea of who I am and who I might
come to be. In my experience, they want to use their energy to help me
create magic, too.

Some might be hesitant to connect with their ancestors either
because they were toxic people, or because they simply didn't know
them. That's fine.

Please know that you don't have to connect with anyone you
don't want to. There are plenty of other connections for you to make
as a witch, like with yourself or with Mother Earth. But you can also
choose a lineage that you were not born into but feel close to, like an
adoptive or found family. You'll also still be able to form a relationship
with ancestors you have never met.

Set up an altar—Create a small space where you can go when you
     want to connect with them. Place photos, heirlooms, or a dish
     of rosemary to create a focus for your altar. I find that keeping a
     candle there and lighting it before I talk/vent to them really sets
     the spiritual tone.

Ask for a hand—If you're having trouble and need outside advice, go
     over to your altar. Ask them a clear question then pull a tarot/
     oracle card to represent their answer. Try to be as objective as
     possible when you interpret it. You can also ask them to join
     in on your spells if you want a magical boost or just some extra
     support while you do your thing.

Do things they'd appreciate—For example, when I want to honor
     my late sister, I visit the beach, which she always loved to do.
     I truly believe she's there by my side enjoying it as much as I

am. In my experience, they appreciate any effort, big or small. However, just living life on your own terms and making the best decisions for you is a way to honor their legacy. You're a part of them and vice versa, so they want nothing more than to see you happy and thriving.

mercury retrograde

When mercury is retrograde, it looks like it is moving backward, but it's not. It's just an illusion—a trick of the eye.

Mercury retrograde only happens a few times a year and lasts a few weeks, but a *lot* of people dread it and the "backward" energy it brings, especially when it comes to things like communications, technology, and travel.

Your school bus could be delayed.

You could accidentally send a sensitive text to the wrong person.

Your laptop or tablet could break at the worst possible moment.

You could have a huge misunderstanding with someone close to you.

You could have an ex-crush or ex-friend show up out of the blue and cause you some confused feelings.

The inconveniences really add up and make it seem like everything that can possibly go wrong *is* going wrong, but that's not actually the case—that's only how it *appears* to you.

I'll be the first to admit that sometimes chaos happens with literally no rhyme or reason; however, in my opinion, the chaos that happens during mercury retrograde is usually the kind of chaos with *purpose*.

Dig a little deeper, and you'll find that it always has something to teach you.

Mercury retrograde gives you the opportunity to move more slowly and to think more carefully about things. It can also emphasize what isn't working too great so you can take some much-needed action.

My advice: stay grounded, do everything with careful thought, and prepare for the worst-case scenario. You'll survive.

feeling overwhelmed by the cycles

Whew.

That was a lot for me to write, so I'm sure it was a lot for you to read.

By now, you might be feeling overwhelmed by how many cycles there are for you to potentially follow. (And I didn't cover anywhere near all of the potential cycles you can live by; this was just a sampling to get you started.)

I know. I've been there.

Here are a few things for you to keep in mind moving forward:

You can incorporate them slowly—When I began my practice, I only celebrated one or two of the Wheel of the Year holidays. As time went on, I slowly began to introduce more when I felt like I could handle them. I get how difficult it can be, especially if you're trying to keep up with all the other holidays, as well as all the other responsibilities in your life.

You don't have to incorporate them at all—Hey, opting out of the cycles entirely and doing magic whenever it feels right to you is okay in my book! Maybe you want to observe some of the cycles and not others. Or maybe you only want to work with certain parts of some cycles and skip the parts you don't vibe with. All of it is valid.

You don't have to observe them all the time—I used to release during every full moon and manifest during every new moon, but that got old really fast since I found that I didn't have things that needed to be released/manifested that often. Now I partake only when I have specific things in mind. I also don't do a prosperity spell every single Thursday, but when I do have a prosperity spell I want to work, I make sure it's *on* Thursday—get it?

You don't have to go all out—You don't have to do a spell for every part of every cycle. Giving it a silent acknowledgment can be enough—so can pulling a tarot card or eating a meal in honor of it. Do whatever you have the energy for. Doing magic when you don't feel like it probably won't be as effective, anyway.

just when she thought there was
no more magic to make,

they opened up their front door
& the twilight sky poured in

to remind her of her own
unending vastness.

—*larger than the whole universe.*

PART IV

more magic

there's always more magic

We've almost reached the end of our time together, but luckily, there's still a little more magic to be made before we say our final goodbye and go our separate ways.

I thought it would be fun to include a few more spells for you to do. This section is intended to be a collection of workings that address things you may deal with in your everyday life—insecurities, self-acceptance, heartbreak. You may not need some of the spells right at this very moment, but there's a chance you will later!

With each working I've also written suggestions for specific cycles I think would make the most sense to align them with. They're merely suggestions, though, not requirements. As with all of the spells in this book, you can do them whenever you feel intuitively called to.

Toward the end of the chapter, you'll find a spread that will come in handy when creating your own spells from scratch. If you'd like, you can jump headfirst into that part, or come back to it whenever you feel ready. (If the very idea of it sounds terrifying to you, then that means it's probably time. Do what scares you.)

spell to banish your insecurities

This is not a spell to banish—or release—the things you're insecure about. That wouldn't be very empowering, would it? Instead, it's a spell intended to banish the feeling of insecurity itself. It won't get rid of your stretchmarks, but it *will* (hopefully) get rid of the shame or embarrassment you feel whenever you look at them. (I highly suggest doing this spell in combination with the next one.)

BEST PERFORMED ON:
Saturday / full moon / Samhain

WHAT YOU'LL NEED:
Your magical journal
A writing utensil

DIRECTIONS:

In your magical journal, write a list of your biggest insecurities. Word each one like "my insecurity about my _____." (This spell is designed for physical traits, but anything that comes to mind will work!)

Once you have your list, read it over.

Afterward, repeat, "I've come to the conclusion that these insecurities no longer serve me. Therefore, they're no longer welcome in my life. Sorry (not sorry), but I just don't have time or energy for any of you anymore. You're hereby banished—*forever*. So mote it be."

Take your writing utensil (preferably a pen or marker to represent permanence) and aggressively scribble out your list. Keep going until you can no longer make out any of the words. Rip into that paper. Have absolutely no mercy as you banish your feelings of insecurity.

Once you're satisfied, rip the page out of your magical journal. Ball it up, stomp on it, ride your bike over it. Throw it out somewhere far away from your house (without littering) so you can make sure you'll never feel any of those things ever again.

spell to accept your "flaws"

For this, you'll need to recall the physical traits you had feelings of insecurity about from the last spell. It's important to do more than just banish them and declare the job done. Your perceived flaws make you uniquely beautiful, so with this spell, you're going to bring in some love and acceptance!

BEST PERFORMED ON:

Friday / new moon / Bealtaine

WHAT YOU'LL NEED:

Red/pink lip gloss (optional—see directions)
Sticky notes
A writing utensil
Your magical journal

DIRECTIONS:

If you have some, apply the red/pink lip gloss to your lips. (If you're not comfortable wearing lip gloss or just don't want to, that's fine. It won't affect the magical energy you're about to create.)

Write out each thing you were once insecure about on its own individual sticky note.

After you write each one, pause to kiss the sticky note (avoiding contact with the ink), and then say, "This part of myself is deserving of love and acceptance, so love and acceptance is what I now give it."

Title a new page in your magical journal with "These parts of myself I have vowed to love and accept, no matter what" and proceed to place the sticky note somewhere on the page. (Don't worry, it doesn't have to look perfect— you can layer them if you have to.)

When you place your last sticky note on the page, say, "So mote it be."

spell to mend your broken heart

Chances are you'll have your heart broken one way or another—whether it's at the hands of a crush, a friend, a family member, an idol, or maybe even yourself. Sometimes your heart will break when a wish goes unfulfilled or when you've lost something important. No matter what your circumstance is, may this spell be much-needed balm for your soul.

BEST PERFORMED ON:
Monday / waning moon / Yule

WHAT YOU'LL NEED:
Red construction paper
Scissors
A small to medium tray
Dried peppermint leaves

DIRECTIONS:

Cut a heart shape out of your red construction paper, small enough to fit comfortably in your tray. (It helps if you fold the piece of paper in half, then draw a half-heart shape starting at the crease and moving up. Cut your way along it, and bam, you have your heart!)

133

Cut a zigzag line down the middle of your paper heart. Place both pieces inside your tray, making sure the halves don't touch.

Gaze upon the heart as you talk everything out. What happened? How does it make you feel? What are your worries and fears moving forward? Cry if you feel called to. (This can be a healing process in and of itself.) Get it all out.

Take each half of the heart and piece them back together. Say, "Though this situation has caused me much pain, I recognize that it has taught me something valuable, even if I can't see it yet. I am choosing to mend it so I can put that lesson into action."

Finally, sprinkle dried peppermint (if you don't have any, you can cut open a peppermint tea bag and use what's inside) over the now whole heart for an extra healing touch. When you're done, say, "So mote it be."

spell to break free from your smartphone

I don't know about you, but when I'm bored, I'll scroll endlessly on my smartphone, laughing at meme after meme. Before I know it, hours have passed. I don't even mean to do it—it almost becomes hypnotic and it's impossible to stop, and I lose sight of real life, which can be disorienting. If you have a smartphone and experience this, too, try this spell to help break free.

BEST PERFORMED ON:
Wednesday / waning moon / Ostara

WHAT YOU'LL NEED:
Your phone
A small drawstring pouch or box
An amethyst crystal

DIRECTIONS:

As soon as you show signs of obsessive phone-scrolling, turn off your phone immediately. (If you want to go the extra mile, then you can cleanse your phone using a bell as soon as it powers down.)

Put your phone into either a drawstring pouch or a box and place it on your altar. Put your amethyst crystal on top—along with all of its other amazing magical properties, it's also used to soothe obsessive behaviors.

Say, "My desire to scroll is gone. From now on, I integrate screen time in a more beneficial way. So mote it be."

Leave your phone there for as long as you're able to. I suggest at least three to five hours, if possible, or even the remainder of the day.

tea spell to calm down

Sometimes I just cannot get a handle on my nerves, so I drink this tea to help me calm down. I find I sleep better if I drink it an hour or so before bedtime, too. Of course, this isn't a replacement for medical treatment (nothing in this book is), so seek that for any ongoing issues related to anxiety or insomnia, and always be sure to reach out to a trusted grown-up in your life!

BEST PERFORMED ON:
Monday / waning moon / Yule / mercury retrograde

WHAT YOU'LL NEED:
Lavender and chamomile tea in a cup
Honey or honey alternative
A spoon

DIRECTIONS:

Prepare your lavender and chamomile tea as directed.

Make sure your space is calm and quiet before you begin—this is true before any spell, but it's especially so for this one.

If you'd like, you can wear something that's soothing to you, like a sweater or a blanket. You may choose to sit on a soft floor pillow, or to hug a cherished stuffed animal friend—whatever helps, right?

Add your honey or honey alternative (e.g., agave or maple syrup) into your tea. As you stir it all together (try to stir in a clockwise motion, as this spell is seeking to *create* calmness), say, "I am calm. I am relaxed. From this point forward, I have complete and total peace of mind. So mote it be."

Sip on your tea in silence. Acknowledge and release any uneasy thoughts that come up.

spell to focus on what matters

Do you ever have a task or something you know you need to do—homework, cleaning your room—but your mind is on just about everything *but* that? Do this spell to persuade it to focus on what matters. (It's also perfect for things like test-taking or giving a presentation in class.)

BEST PERFORMED ON:
Wednesday / waxing moon / Imbolg

WHAT YOU'LL NEED:
A small to medium tray
The Knight of Swords tarot card
Five to six small rainbow fluorite crystals

DIRECTIONS:

In the middle of your tray, lay down your Knight of Swords tarot card. (This knight in particular has a reputation for setting their sights on an idea and charging toward it—the exact energy you want as a result of this spell!)

Arrange your rainbow fluorite crystals in a circle surrounding your knight.

Sit and concentrate on the contents of the tray for a few moments—give your spell as much *focused* energy as you possibly can. Do this for, say, three to five minutes. (Think of it like a meditation with a specific magical purpose.)

Next, say this affirmation: "All of my attention is focused on (task at hand) for (time frame). I get done what I need to get done in the timeliest and most efficient manner. As I do so, I am ever-calm, never stressed. The results are quality, not just quantity. So mote it be."

You might want to pluck one of the crystals from the tray and keep it with you as you go about your task!

spell to own your amazingness

Confession: I still get imposter syndrome about being an author. I've been on bestseller lists, I've won awards, I've had sold-out readings . . . yet I still go through periods when I doubt my abilities and convince myself that I don't deserve any of this. If you ever go through similar moments of self-doubt, do this spell to own your amazingness!

BEST PERFORMED ON:
Tuesday / full moon / Bealtaine

WHAT YOU'LL NEED:
Your magical journal
A writing utensil
A piece of scrap paper
A locket necklace

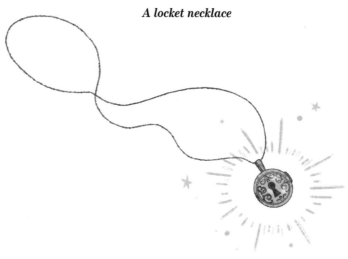

DIRECTIONS:

Take out your magical journal and describe yourself like you're the main character in an epic fantasy novel. What are you known for? What are your accomplishments? Don't be afraid to mix fact with fiction or brag a little.

Now take your scrap paper (it should be a small piece) and write down your favorite line from this description—the one that makes you feel unstoppable, the one that makes you feel good about being *you*.

Roll—or fold—your scrap paper as tiny as you need it to be, and then tuck it into the locket and close it back up.

Hold the necklace in your hands as you say, "I am no imposter. I am exactly what I say I am: (the line from your self-description). No one and nothing can ever take that away from me, not even myself. So mote it be."

Now you have a necklace that acts as a forever reminder that you're amazing!

spell for self-forgiveness

The fact is that we're all humans and we're all capable of making mistakes; however, sometimes it can be difficult to cope with this. A better use of your energy would be to accept what you've done and learn to live with it. (Note: this is *not* an alternative to taking accountability.)

BEST PERFORMED ON:

Friday / waning moon / Imbolg

WHAT YOU'LL NEED:
Your magical journal
A writing utensil
An envelope
Lavender sprigs
Tape

DIRECTIONS:

In your magical journal, I want you to write a letter forgiving yourself for your mistake—not excusing, *forgiving*. There is a huge difference. Make sure you include some plans to rectify your mistake (if needed/possible) and do better moving forward.

Once you're done, read this letter aloud to yourself. Take the paper out of your journal, fold it up, and put it in your envelope. Address the envelope to yourself (you can put your full address or just write your name on the front) and seal it.

After, take your lavender sprigs and tape them to the front of the envelope. (I find that lavender has a very gentle and forgiving energy.)

Hold the letter in your hands and say, "Self-compassion is beautiful, and I hereby give it to myself freely and without restraint. No longer do I punish myself for chapters long closed, for chapters that cannot be rewritten. Self, know that I forgive you for your missteps; even if you can't make this situation right, know that you still have time to make better decisions. So mote it be."

spell for luck

We all need an extra pinch of luck sometimes. This is a spell I would do if I were, say, trying to increase my odds of being cast in the school play, making the sports team, or otherwise hoping things go my way (for the good of all and with harm to none). I hope this can help you, too!

BEST PERFORMED ON:
Thursday / new moon / any harvest holiday

WHAT YOU'LL NEED:
A green candle in a holder
A symbol of what you need luck for
A lucky personal item (optional)
A lighter or match

DIRECTIONS:

Put your green candle in the middle of your spellwork space.

To one side of the candle, place a symbol of what you need luck for, like a copy of a script or a tennis ball. (If you don't have anything, write down a description of what you want.)

To the other side of the candle, place your lucky personal item, if using. Perhaps you have a lucky crystal, a lucky scrunchie, or even the cliché lucky pair of socks. I won't judge no matter what it is.

Light your candle. Close your eyes. Imagine in detail what it would be like to have this situation go in your favor. Make sure you bring that feeling in when you say, "I am so overjoyed now that I have _____. I truly am lucky, and may I forever be." Say this three times total, tying it up with "So mote it be."

Let your candle burn down, if possible. Wait and see what happens.

water bowl spell to be a happy witch

Do you ever just feel like you need a little positivity boost? Do this water bowl spell to help coax out the happy witch within. (This is definitely *not* intended to treat or cure serious emotional issues. This spell is meant for lighthearted occasions only.) Added bonus: some happy energy for your room/space, too!

BEST PERFORMED ON:
Sunday / a full or new moon / Litha

WHAT YOU'LL NEED:
A small to medium bowl
Tap water
Orange slices
Three cinnamon sticks
A handful of whole cloves
A spoon

DIRECTIONS:

Fill your bowl about halfway with tap water.

To the water, add your orange slices (for happiness and joy), cinnamon sticks (for warmth and energy), and cloves (to protect against negative energy).

Stir the bowl clockwise as you say, "I am a happy witch. This is my happy space. No negative energy may here pace. So mote it be."

Set the bowl on your altar. Sit in front of it and focus on the water for a few minutes, making a point to think nothing but happy thoughts.

If you'd like, you may leave it on your altar for a few hours so it can fill your room/space with happy energy, too.

When you're done, go ahead and drain your bowl. Toss or compost the ingredients.

hot chocolate spell for anything you want

This spell is extremely versatile and can be used for anything you want (like the title suggests), as hot chocolate has properties that energize any magical intention you give it. It's especially good for things you want to happen quickly—like, *right now*. Consider this a step toward creating your own spells.

BEST PERFORMED ON:
Any given day

WHAT YOU'LL NEED:
A cup of hot chocolate
A spoon or stirrer
Powdered cinnamon (optional)

DIRECTIONS:

The first step is as simple as it gets: start by making a cup of hot chocolate using a premade powder mix. Be sure to follow the instructions on the packet or box.

As you stir the powder and liquid together (clockwise to manifest, counterclockwise to banish), say your affirmation. It can be something like "I make it through this day stronger than ever before" (manifesting) or "I am amazing at dissolving all the challenges that come my way today" (banishing). Personalize it for *your* day.

If you have powdered cinnamon, you can add a few shakes on top as you say, "So mote it be." Because of cinnamon's fiery energy, it will energize your intention even further!

creating your own spell

Alright, the time has finally come for you to create your own spell! Refer to the magical journal prompts below when you have a topic in mind. You have no reason to be nervous. You've learned so much through reading and doing—all that's left is to implement it!

- Why are you doing this spell? What is it that you hope to achieve by casting it?

- Do you want to *manifest* or *banish* something? (If you're not trying to make something go away—or banish it—then you're probably trying to create something, aka manifest it.)

- When are you going to do your spell? Using a combination of your witchy knowledge and intuition, decide based on what makes the most sense. (A certain day of the week? A moon phase? A Wheel of the Year holiday?)

- Which tools will you use? This can mean crystals, herbs, candles, cards, or other magical-to-you objects. Even if you're simply intuitively drawn to something, put into words why you've chosen it. Don't include things just to include them; sometimes simpler *is* better.

Prewrite an affirmation to include in your spell. Don't be thoughtless with this; really spend some time on this part because it's what everything else in your spell will revolve around. Empower and encourage yourself with your words, and don't forget to word your intention as though it's already happened.

Which action will you take along with your words? You can do any combination of things, such as making a list, lighting a candle, or crafting a spell jar. If applicable, you might want to move in a clockwise circle to manifest or a counterclockwise circle to banish.

Once your spell is finished, draw an illustration of what it looked like. (Or a few, depending on how many steps there were.) You don't need to be an artist to do this—this is just to help you if you ever plan to repeat the spell in the future.

How did it go? Self-reflect on how you feel about your spell immediately after, a week after, a month after, and even a year after. What were the short-term results? What about the long-term results? Is there anything you'd like to do differently next time?

so this is "goodbye"

Though this particular book is now coming to an end, I beg you not to let it be the end of your magical journey.

Let it be merely the beginning.

As you move forward on your path, you're almost certainly going to experience periods when you feel unmotivated to do spellwork or even forget that you have magic altogether. This happens to the most experienced witches, even the lifelong ones.

Yes, even to me.

When—*not if*—it happens to you, don't fret too much, for your magic will always be there when you're ready to find it again. Instead, use that energy to embrace your magical lulls. See them for what they are: an opportunity to rest before your next powerful chapter.

Keep this book close. The second you begin to feel lost, crack it open again and go back to page 1. Immerse yourself in these words. Seek bits of inspiration wherever you can. Remember your own unique inner moondust and perform one of my simple spells, or better yet, use them to inspire one of your own creation.

You can do this every year, if you'd like. Start a few weeks before Yule and slowly make your way back through all four parts. See the first spell as a rededication ritual of sorts where you remember—or add onto—your ethics as well as your magic.

~~Goodbye.~~

See you some other time, whether it's within these pages or in brand-new ones.

Laced with love,

amanda

As we say so long for now, it's also time for you to say goodbye to the person you were before you decided to be a witch—all of the old beliefs that no longer serve you, all of those old self-limitations. Get out your magical journal and write a heartfelt letter thanking past-you for everything that led up to that moment, and the way this decision has (hopefully) improved your mindset and life.

special acknowledgments

My poet-spouse, Parker Lee—Thank you for listening to my dreams and for giving me the space as well as the support I needed as I slowly brought them to life. The spearmint lattes were a huge help, too. <3

My literary agent, Lauren Spieller—Thank you for believing I could write a book like this and be successful at it. Without you and your tireless work, it wouldn't have found the amazing home it did. You're the BEST!

My RP team—Thank you not just for agreeing to publish this but for your incredible enthusiasm surrounding my work. It couldn't possibly be in better hands.

My beta readers—Thank you Christine Day, Summer Webb, and Mira Kennedy for following me through the genre shift and for the honest feedback that helped this book become the best possible book it could be.

My friends and family—Thank you to those who are forever cheering me on, regardless of what I decide to write.

My readers—Thank you, thank you, thank you!!! Just the fact that you would take a chance on my words means all the stars in the sky to me. I hope this book made you believe in your ability to make all of your dreams come true; if not, then I hope it will at least look really pretty on your bookshelf.

My illustrator, Raquel Aparicio—Thank you for the most magical illustrations a witchy writer could ask for!

about the author

amanda lovelace (she/they) is the bestselling author of several books & decks, & she is now the author of the book you hold in your hands, *Your Magical Life*. When they aren't reading, writing, or drinking a much-needed cup of coffee, you can find them casting spells from their home in a (very) small town on the Jersey Shore, where they reside with their poet-spouse & their three cats.

follow amanda

amandalovelace.com